Homilies for the **Whole Community**

Wisdom from a Pastor's Heart

YEAR C

REVEREND MICHAEL T. HAYES

Kathleen M. Groh, General Editor

TWENTY
THIRD 23rd
PUBLICATIONS

The celtic artwork in this volume was drawn by Joe Pfahl, a long-time friend of Fr. Michael T. Hayes. His artwork can be seen at www.joegravity.com. The ox is a reproduction from the Book of Kells depicting the Gospel of Luke.

Twenty-Third Publications
A Division of Bayard
One Montauk Avenue, Suite 200
New London, CT 06320
(860) 437-3012 or (800) 321-0411
www.23rdpublications.com

ISBN-10: 1-58595-568-X
ISBN 978-1-58595-568-8
Library of Congress Catalog Card Number: 2006923592
Printed in the U.S.A.

Contents

Advent & Christmas

Lent & Easter

Ordinary Time

Other Feasts & Occasions

Fr. Michael T. Hayes

Michael T. Hayes was born in Lahinch, Co. Clare, Ireland. As he liked to say, he was "the only child (unspoiled) of Margaret and Michael Hayes." He spent his youth on Ireland's west coast beaches and as a caddy at the world-famous Lahinch National Golf Course. The love of the game never left him. The family later moved to Brosna and he attended high school at St. Flannan's in Ennis, Ireland.

After earning top scholastic honors and completing seminary at St. Patrick's, Carlow, Ireland, he was ordained for the Diocese of Duluth, Minnesota on June 10, 1960, where he served in parish ministry for forty-three years. He claimed "Life, Be in It" as his motto and became well-known for his non-judgmental approach to ministry, his sense of humor, and his generosity.

Fr. Mike was a gifted storyteller and a lover of literature, poetry, theater, and music. Irish culture permeated his ministry. Fr. Hayes was the founder and pastor of Holy Angels Catholic Church in Moose Lake, Minnesota, and served this community for seventeen years. After Father Mike's brief, courageous struggle with cancer, parishioners and friends from all walks of life celebrated the life and death of this perfectly outrageous, witty, and wise shepherd on August 11, 2003.

Foreword

God made people because God loves stories. In many ways effective parish ministry is anchored in a pastor who lives and tells a story of Jesus and how his love can be at the heart of our own story.

This is a wonderful collection of homilies from a superb storyteller who is lifted from the shores of Lake Wobegon. His stories are also lifted from the shores of Lake Galilee. They resonate with the wisdom and energy of a Holy Land experience where a parish community in Moose Lake, Minnesota, becomes a living people who are eucharistic and alive. Lake Wobegon and Lake Galilee do come together in Moose Lake.

I have read many collections of sermons in my forty-three years as a pastor and priest. This is the most authentic sermon book I have ever opened. It is poetic and wise and humorous. It is focused. And it inspires a dedicated pastor to develop a conversation and a time of storytelling in preparing for a community gathered to celebrate life in Christ.

The Hasidim have a story about a young disciple who said to the holy one, "You know when I study and join in the grand feasts, I experience great light and life during it. But it all disappears when the feast is over...everything dies in me."

The old holy one replied, "It is just this feeling when a person walks through the woods at night. The air is delicious and the breeze is cool. If another joins the traveler with a lantern, they can walk safely and joyfully together. But if they come to a crossroads and the one with the lantern departs, then the first must grope his way alone unless he carries the light within himself."

The homilies of Fr. Mike leave me with light and direction. The resurrected Lord did not change the world; it is as dark as ever. But the Lord did change the apostles. We must be risen people.

These are homilies for a risen people. They are absolutely wonderful and great fun to read. They also meet us where we are. It is said that God meets us where we are, but finding ourselves where we are is always the hardest part. For that we need others.

This rare and wonderful collection of homilies has enabled me to rediscover where I am and also points me in exciting ways to where God is meeting me today. This is the kind of book with appeal to all of God's people: Catholic, Protestant, Evangelical, charismatic, traditional, experimental. This is a rare gift to all of us from the heart of Fr. Mike, a priest who was "alive behind the eyeballs," and whose thoughts invite us to the fullness of life.

—Rev. Ralph Peterson, New York, NY
(Rev. Harold Peterson, Ralph's father, served as chaplain with Fr. Hayes at Mercy Hospital and Minnesota State Correctional Facility)

Holey, Wholly, Holy

We had just finished thoroughly cleaning the old rectory at St. Francis in Carlton, Minnesota, on a hot summer afternoon. Our pastor was leaving and we were anticipating his short-term replacement. As we were sipping sodas, we heard voices coming through the back door.

Fr. Joe Hughes walked in and peering in shyly behind him was a tall, slightly slouching young priest with rumpled clothes. After introductions, he asked in a deep Irish brogue what everyone did for the parish. I was in a bit of a panic because everyone else had an official title like president of the Rosary Society, secretary, housekeeper; then my turn came. I simply said, "I'm the minister of hospitality." Fr. Michael Hayes' blue eyes lit up in delight.

I must admit that I had no idea what "minister of hospitality" would mean in his life nor mine when I took on the position, but I did think my first role was to "unrumple" him, so I offered to do his laundry. He basically had a few golf clothes, one black shirt, and a suit that he "borrowed" from Bishop Casey in Patterson, New Jersey. He would say that he had "anticipated the bishop's generosity."

I soon found that his cigarette smoking was going to be his nemesis. From his car seats, golf shirts, sweaters, to his polyester pants, he had holes in everything he owned. An ugly, blue herringbone pair of pants was particularly "holey." At one of the washings, I just hung them on the line and figured that if he didn't get those wretched things back, he wouldn't even miss them. He never said a thing.

Toward the end of the summer, a good friend and fellow parishioner asked me if I wanted to put anything in her garage sale; I scooped up the pants and thought, "Good riddance." That afternoon, I heard a car door slam in the driveway and looked out. There, on the drive stood the pastor of St. Francis, wearing none other than the "holey pants" that he claimed he found in the thrift store!

Goodness knows I wasn't the only woman in his many parishes that tried to make Fr. Mike a bit more presentable. Fully dressed he could look unmatched and wrinkled in five minutes. He once remarked that "If someone has to recognize that I am a priest by the clothes I wear, I'm not a very good one."

"Wholly" described Fr. Mike's ministry. It was inclusive of everyone from the prisoners in the Moose Lake Correctional Facility to the elderly in the nursing homes of Carlton and Moose Lake. He had ministry connections to the very famous and to the traveler who slipped off the freeway looking for a handout and gas money.

He was wholly present to all of his parishioners, young and old, even the ones he had left behind when he moved on to a new parish. He never stopped being our pastor because he entered our lives deeply and sincerely, bringing the presence of Christ in words and actions.

Fr. Mike was with us in our happiest times, whether it was in a local restaurant, gala events at the church, or in the Knappogue Castle in Ireland. He was there for great food and good company. Be it baptisms, first communions, confirmations, or weddings, he brought with him profound thoughts and prayers and sprinkled them with humor for good measure.

I think our most heartfelt times came when we struggled with grief and pain from sickness or death of spouses, children, parents, and grandparents. His homilies were carefully chosen, written and delivered with gentle compassion, but with firm conviction in the resurrection. Not only that, he remained long after the crowds left, even if only through a quick phone call at just the right moment. He let people know that they were being remembered.

The last word "holy" means "coming from God." We were blessed by God with Fr. Mike's gifted presence among us. With his great love of literature, he took delight in creatively and skillfully playing with words and ideas. His weekly homilies were poetic treasures. He never once complained or bemoaned the fact that he had to get ready for Sunday. Instead, he would sit in his favorite diner booth late into Friday evening until he had a fresh and challenging homily for his community.

By the time I moved to the Twin Cities in 1988, I was a parishioner and friend of Fr. Mike. Soon after, the homilies began to arrive every Wednesday. The envelope would be stuffed not only with the hand-written homily, but with newspaper clippings, jokes, Irish publications, and anything he discovered in his briefcase that he found interesting. I stored the homilies in boxes that soon began to stack up. Some I took to my office and used for presentations on Eucharist and reconciliation. Many of them I shared with staff members for Bible study and with the parish RCIA team. For thirteen years I collected these homilies.

After Fr. Mike's death in August 2003, I spent the next lenten season putting the homilies in notebooks. One morning I e-mailed Bill Huebsch of Twenty-Third Publications and asked if he had any ideas about publishing them. His response was "Send me one." The return e-mail was "They are poetry!" Soon after, we met for lunch and this great adventure began.

With Bill's encouragement, the consent of Fr. Mike's cousins, and the help of faithful and talented friends, I have chosen sixty-one homilies for the lectionary Year C that reveal the heart and mind of a truly holy man. The homilies have been authentically re-created in style and color. He wrote them to be proclaimed, so the movement of the words and the emphasis could be seen as he preached. Sprinkled among them are anecdotes and stories from his many friends. These give you a glimpse into the life and personality of this unique priest.

I hope you enjoy and are moved by these treasured homilies as you read and ponder them. But it is my greatest desire that you find places to use these homilies, in part or totally, and proclaim them in your ministry to the whole community.

This collection of homilies is dedicated to my daughter with a grateful heart.
Therese Ann
Stunning beauty
Wonderfully witty and wise
Lover of horses, greyhounds, and Jim
Writer

—Kathleen M. Groh

Advent &
Christmas

Jer 33:14–16; 1 Thess 3:12—4:2; Luke 21:25–28, 34–36

No One Is Coming

The season of Advent is like the ancient God of Rome, Janus,
    for whom the month of January is named.
Janus is depicted in art as having two faces.
One face looks backward into the past,
    the other looks forward into the future.

The season of Advent is like that.
It looks backward into the past to the first coming of Christ,
    and it looks forward into the future for the second coming of Christ.

And so today we stand at the midpoint
    between the two great moments of history,
    and we hear again the invitation of the Scriptures
on this first Sunday of Advent:

"Stand up and raise your heads,
    because your redemption is drawing near." (Luke 21:28)
"Be on guard." (Luke 21:34)
"Be alert at all times." (Luke 21:36)

I recently read a book called *A Nation of Victims*.
It talks about the tendency of people
    to blame their problems
        on anything, or anyone, other than themselves.

For example,
if a person is a thief,
    it is because he/she grew up in poverty
        or was born with a predisposition to steal.

If a person commits murder,
    it is because he/she is suffering from a condition called
        "urban survival syndrome."

All are victims of their genetic make up
    and the way they were reared.
An opposite view of human behavior
    argues that all persons are totally responsible for their conduct.
Regardless of their parents, and environment,
    people can still become solid citizens if they choose to do so.
If they become less than that, it is their own fault.
This position is usually argued by persons
    who were born into
        and grew up in fortunate circumstances.

Obviously, neither of these theories is correct in and of itself.

The notion that we are only victims is not the whole truth,
    and the notion that all persons
    are entirely responsible for themselves
        is not true either.

To get the whole truth,
    both of these partial insights must be put together.
Whatever life deals for us
    or to us, you and I still have a choice.

We can take a fortunate circumstance
    and waste it, just throw it away.
We can take an unfortunate circumstance
    and do something decent with it.

After heredity and environment have done their utmost,
    we still get to vote on how our lives will turn out.

Our gospel today contains both aspects.
It begins with Jesus painting a grim picture of life for the disciples.

He was talking about a hard circumstance in which to live.
In this sense, the disciples were victims.
They did not choose the hard circumstance.
    It was simply given to them.

But having painted the grim picture, Jesus went on to say,
    "Now when these things begin to take place,
        stand up and raise your heads,
        because your redemption is drawing near." (Luke 21:28)

When life is hard, we still have a choice.
We can lie down and quit
    or we can stand up to life
        and deal with it as it comes.

The first thing we must do
    is take responsibility for ourselves,
    as in the verse of a well-known Kenny Roger's song:
"You've got to know when to hold them,
know when to fold them,
    know when to walk away,
    and know when to run."

A psychologist working with clients
    had a phrase framed and hung it on his wall.
It said, "No one is coming."

He stressed the fact that nothing is going to improve
unless the clients take responsibility
    for their own thoughts, feelings, and actions.

It means that no one will come and fix us
    nor do everything for us while we do nothing.
He encouraged his clients
    to take ownership for what was
    happening in their own lives.

One day a client challenged him about the saying, "No one is coming."
He pointed to it and said, "It's not true! You came!"
The psychologist said, "Well, you came is correct,
     but I came to say that no one is coming."

The coming of Christ does not mean
     that he does everything for us and we do nothing.

Christ is coming, but not to dispense us from responsibility for ourselves.
Just the opposite.

In the words of the gospel, we are invited
     to "be on guard, be alert at all times." (Luke 21:34)

Luke mentions specific things and the
     "worries of this life that can catch you unexpectedly, like a trap."
     (Luke 21:34–35)
What a terrific image!
So often we hear people say, "I feel trapped."
If we feel trapped,
     we have to practice self-responsibility
     and release ourselves from the trap.
"No one is coming" to do it for us.

As adults we can't just blame
     the economy for our lack of funds
     our parents for our dysfunction
     our church for our lack of compassion.

God insists that we do our part.

Advent is a time for us to say,
"No one is coming," but I am becoming more like Christ.

Let us say during this season of conspicuous consumption:
I believe in becoming more than I have been in the past.
I believe in Advent.

A Glimpse of Fr. Hayes

It was Advent. The Christmas preparations were hectic, and the lack of funds left me with the feeling of being buried alive. I decided to receive the sacrament of reconciliation with the children during their faith formation classes.

When I had finished with my litany of woes, Fr. Mike gently talked about getting my priorities right. He asked me to focus on Mary who said "yes" to giving birth to a baby when none of the circumstances on the outside seemed right. Mary kept her priorities in order. Fr. Mike helped me to focus on mine and has made every Christmas thereafter much more meaningful.

—Irene Mckay, parishioner of St. Francis and Holy Trinity, Barnum, MN

Bar 5:1–9; Phil 1:4–6, 8–11; Luke 3:1–6

Turn Around

What are we to do with Advent?
It's too important to ignore, and yet it is difficult to observe it properly.

Some parishioners even complain
    when the singing of Christmas hymns is delayed until December 24th.
The parish that is strict about the celebration of Advent
    seems out of step with the rest of the world.

In the wilderness of eighteen shopping days left, we hear,
    "the voice of one crying out in the wilderness:
        'Prepare the way of the Lord.'" (Luke 3:4)

John the Baptist,
    who would probably be considered a weirdo in our day,
    comes upon the scene with urgent words,
        "Prepare the way of the Lord." (Luke 3:4)

It is the human way of things
    that we are often taken by surprise.
The unexpected breaks into our comfortable complacency;
margins blur and fade;
    an untraveled world looms.
Advent is here to alert us all to the presence of the unexpected.

Who is this strange figure
    that the gospel brings to our doorsteps this morning?
We didn't expect such a visitation
    for he is dressed in outlandish gear:
        a garment of camel hair, a leather belt around his waist.
Dare we invite him in?

We must,
    because he is the one possessed and on fire with the Word of God!
He is the great Advent figure.
"A voice crying in the wilderness"
    is how he describes himself.

But the wilderness has always been a safe distance from here,
    we say.
Yet, the unexpected breaks into our lives,
    and we are taken by surprise.

Now, today, in this place of God, we find that the wilderness is right here.
It is within and around us in our forgetfulness of God.
Ours is a sinful world, full of sinful people,
    and the wilderness is as contemporary
    as our own lived experience.

As Paul once reminded the Philippians,
    the wilderness is only overcome with
        knowledge and insight into the ways of Christ.

John the Baptist, too, offers us a way to face the wilderness.
He preached a fiery word,
    "the baptism of repentance for the forgiveness of sins." (Luke 3:3)

In Greek, repentance means
"turning around and facing another direction."
It's not just casually saying, "I'm sorry,"
    or "pardon me."
It is a deep awareness of the need we have
    for God's cleansing presence in our lives.

Because we continue to fail,
    repentance is a daily experience for us Christians.
God's faithful love and mercy reach out to us everyday.
No wonder we begin our worship with confession and absolution.
This is the only way we can approach a holy and gracious God.

Let me give you one dramatic example of the meaning of repentance.

As you know, in the late 1980s, Americans were held hostage in Lebanon.
Perhaps the best known of the hostages was Terry Anderson,
    an Associated Press journalist.
He was kidnapped in 1985 and imprisoned for 2,454 days,
    almost seven years.

At first he was blindfolded most of the time and held in chains.
He was losing his capacity to think.
When asked what he wanted, he replied that he wanted a Bible.
An object thumped onto his bed.
He removed his blindfold and found a Bible.
He began to read, starting with Genesis.

Terry Anderson was raised a Catholic,
    but had not been practicing his faith for years.
That Bible was like a gift from heaven.
He read, and read, and thought about his life.
He had lots of time to think.
He wanted to confess that he had hurt his first wife and daughter.
He wanted to confess his many mistakes and his arrogance.
He wasn't sure that people liked him
    and he certainly didn't like himself very much.

Later in the first year of his captivity,
Terry Anderson became aware
    that other hostages were living next door.
One was a priest—Fr. Lawrence Jenko.

Terry asked the guard if he could see the priest
    so he could make a confession.
His captors agreed, and Fr. Jenko came to Terry Anderson's room.
Both men took off their blindfolds.
It was twenty-five years since he had made a confession.
Fr. Jenko gently encouraged him.
Terry Anderson began telling the priest of his sins.

There was much to confess:
    a bad marriage, chasing other women, drinking.

It was a tremendously emotional experience.
When he had finished, both Terry and Fr. Jenko were in tears.
Fr. Jenko then laid his right hand upon Anderson's head
    and proclaimed,
"In the name of a gently loving God, you are forgiven."

This was a turning point in Terry Anderson's life.
    He had turned around and was facing in another direction.

His faith deepened.
He had begun the process of
    leaving the darkness and facing the light.
That is what repentance is like.

"Prepare the way of the Lord." (Luke 3:4)
John the Baptist calls on each of us
    to stop in the middle of our frantic preparation for Christmas
        to hear the message of Advent.

"The voice of one crying out in the wilderness:
'Prepare the way of the Lord,
    make his paths straight.
Every valley shall be filled,
    and every mountain and hill
        shall be made low,
    and the crooked shall be made straight,
    and the rough ways made smooth;
    and all flesh shall see the
        salvation of God.'" (Luke 3:4–6)

Zeph 3:14–18a; Phil 4:4–7; Luke 3:10–18

What Then Should We Do?

The great events of history can be roughly divided into two categories:
> those that are interesting and nothing more
> and others, that are not only interesting,
>> but also call for some kind of response.

For example, we know that in 1945, a golfer named Bryan Nelson
> won eleven consecutive professional tournaments.
He did that almost fifty years ago,
> and no golfer, before or since,
> has ever even come close to duplicating that feat.

That is an interesting bit of history,
but none of us feel any need to do anything about it.

On the other hand,
> we know that in 1955, a scientist named Jonas Salk
> discovered a vaccine that would stop the spread of polio.
That bit of history is much more than interesting.
It obligated people around the world to immunize their families,
> and to share this vaccine with the rest of the world.
and thus this dread disease
has been virtually eliminated from the earth.

Some great events are merely interesting.
Other great events are compelling.
We have to do something about them.

There is no doubt in which of the two categories Advent belongs.
It is endlessly fascinating to know
> that God has come into the world in the person of Jesus.

It is even more fascinating to know
　　that he keeps coming into our lives
　　　　day after day, year after year.

But this historic event, this ongoing event,
　　is much more than interesting.
It is obligating.

Our gospel reading for today highlights this aspect of Advent.
John the Baptist had been preaching in the Jordan River valley,
　　proclaiming the coming of the Lord.
The people were captivated by his message.
But those who truly believed were more than interested.
They became involved.
They felt a need to respond to this event.

When John had finished preaching,
　　the crowd gathered around him and said:
　　　　"What then should we do?" (Luke 3:10)

This was and still is
　　the appropriate response to the coming of Christ,
　　　　the greatest event in all of history.
God has come to live among us and be known by us.

We cannot just go on with business as usual;
　　we need to do something.
　　　　"What then should we do?" (Luke 3:10)

What are we waiting for?
Whom are we expecting?

We are waiting for Christmas.
We are expecting Jesus.
Yet, Jesus is here, isn't he?

He lives!

First, he lives in all the world.
He is everywhere
    in every nook and cranny of the world.
He has to be because he is God the Son.

Second, he lives in this church building
    in the tabernacle as the Bread of Life.
I know he is here
    as truly as you and I are here:
        body, blood, soul, and divinity.

Third, Jesus lives within us, each of us,
    each and every moment, waking or sleeping,
    as long as we love him,
    as long as we have faith in his Last Supper promises.

If in Advent
    you do not experience him here
    or in your world,
    in your home,
    or in your flesh and spirit,
    then do not look for him in the crib at Christmas.
You will not find him there.
    "What then should we do?"

You may have missed these words fifteen minutes ago,
    hidden in the opening prayer of the Mass:
    "Lord God, may we, your people,
        who look forward to the birth of Christ,
        experience the joy of salvation."

Experience it.
The heart of Advent is a single word,
Experience.

Jesus lives.

Mic 5:1–4a; Heb 10:5–10; Luke 1:39–45

Why Has This Happened To Me?

So much of the way we celebrate Christ's coming
is wrapped up (pardon the pun) in giving and receiving gifts.

We make lists, and we begin shopping long before Christmas
to find just the right present for each person.
Advertisers and media merchants
compete for our attention with their own versions
of what is called the "Christmas Spirit."

The real issue and true presents or true presence of the season
awaits our discovery.

Every week,
the believing community is gifted with the sacred liturgy:
the rites, the readings, the prayers,
the psalms, the songs, the gestures.
All grace us with an ever new discovery of God's ways and works.

Key to unwrapping the gift of the Word for this Fourth Sunday of Advent
is the simple question of Mary's cousin Elizabeth:
"And why has this happened to me,
that the mother of my Lord comes to me?" (Luke 1:43)

Each Advent, Elizabeth's question
calls each of us to ponder anew
the gift of God's presence among us
in the least likely places, in the least likely people,
in the most unlikely ways, until he comes.

Our gospel for today reports what may have been the first Christmas party.
The guest list was quite small.
Only two people attended, both were women.
There were four really, but two were not yet born.

One woman was named Elizabeth
     who would soon give birth to John the Baptist,
     and the other was Mary.
She had just learned that she would soon have a son, also.
He would be the Savior of the world.

The most striking thing about their party was the tone of it.
Mary was happy for Elizabeth, and Elizabeth was happy for Mary.
And both of them were grateful to God.

It was time to celebrate,
     and these two women did exactly that.

They shouted.
They sang.
And we can assume that
     they laughed, danced, and embraced.

It was party time.
Elizabeth was so happy
     that she was sure her unborn baby was happy, too.

And what was it that these two women were celebrating?
Mary and Elizabeth,
     for all their primitive lifestyle,
     were way ahead of us on this score.
Their God was not absent but present,
     not passive but active.
God was at work in their lives and in their world.

They had felt God's presence.
They had heard God's voice.
They had witnessed God's deeds
    and that, for them, was sufficient cause for celebration.

Mary and Elizabeth had literally given themselves to God,
    and God, through Mary, was giving the world God's Son.
So the concept of giving goes right to the heart of the matter.
That is the reason behind the tradition
    of exchanging gifts at this time of year.

God has given to us,
    and now we celebrate by giving,
        and it needn't be something we've purchased in a store.

I have in mind the kind of gift
    that Mary and Elizabeth gave;
        they gave themselves.
So we can give of ourselves
    to each other and to God.

I suggest we try giving a little gladness this Christmas.
You have enough that you can share it,
    and you will be surprised how your supply will grow.

Don't be economical with your smiles.
Don't hoard your laughter.
Don't be a miser with your praise.
Don't be too tired to play with your children.

Give something of spiritual value
    and realize that God is working through you
    as he did with Mary and Elizabeth.

Who will God love through you today?
Who will God encourage by what you say?

Who will God bless by what you do?
Whose hope will God renew through you today?

If you recall this as you begin each day,
    you will be alert to the possibilities
        that are presented to you all week long.

Only you can respond as you offer the people you meet
    your unique Christmas gift of love just as Elizabeth did.
Your words will be:
    "Why has this happened to me
        that God has sent my Lord to me?"

I'll end with this familiar song from the Fantastiks:
"Try to remember when life was so tender,
    that no one wept except the willow.
Try to remember when life was so tender,
    that dreams were kept beside your pillow.
Try to remember when life was so tender,
    that love was an ember about to billow.
Try to remember, and if you remember,
    then follow."

Isa 62:11–12; Titus 3:4–7; Luke 2:15–20

That's Christmas!

"Well, it's been a quiet week in Lake Wobegon."
With these familiar words, Garrison Keillor
    begins one of his homespun stories on Minnesota Public Radio,
    and it is enough to prime us
        to hear another tale of warmth and humor.

We begin to smile before we even hear the story
    because every time, we are moved to reach into the past
        and remember some experience of our own.
There is a sense in which everyone of us
    is from the fictional town of Lake Wobegon.

If we don't know the people who gossip a bit at the Chatterbox Cafe,
    we certainly know others like them and places like that.
We know Father Emil and Pastor Inkvist,
    and we laugh and cry with the men, women, and children of that place
        —which actually doesn't exist—
        or which perhaps is really every place.

Some of us are from real towns like Lake Wobegon;
    towns with funny names or an unlikely history.
Some of these places never seem to be significant,
    except to the people who happen to live there,
    like the village of Brosna in Ireland,
        where I lived with my parents for a short time.

Jesus came from a place like that.
You may remember that incident in John's gospel
    where Nathaniel ridicules Nazareth,
        the place where Jesus lived.

Philip had urged him to come to meet Jesus,
    but Nathaniel scoffingly remarked,
    "Can any good come out of Nazareth?"
Yes, perhaps Nazareth was a "Wobegon" kind of place.
Today's gospel mentions another Wobegon kind of place,
    Bethlehem.

In the time of the prophet Micah,
    Bethlehem was "too small to be named among the clans of Judah."

If you were naming the important places,
    important enough to regard their inhabitants as a clan of the nation,
Bethlehem certainly would not have been among them.
It was not important enough.

Christmas is the feast of the Inappropriate and the Unexpected.
As this world thinks,
    you would not expect God to be born in a stable,
    or to live to be a friend of sinners,
    or to die among thieves.

As far as this world goes, you might not expect God at all,
but God came
    in the flesh.
That's Christmas.

Our inappropriate, unexpected God turns up
    in an unexpected way,
    in an unexpected place,
    in an unexpected form.

That's Christmas, real Christmas,
God with us.

Jesus is the Lord of the Borrowed:
  a borrowed birthplace,
  a borrowed death place,
  a borrowed manger,
  and a borrowed tomb.

But the borrower comes lending,
  lending grace and meaning to poverty,
    and all that goes with it,
    and all that goes without.

Like all babies, this baby tends to stand the world on its head,
  to ask for unreasonable sacrifice,
  to give unreasonable delight.
Unreasonable except that love,
  real love,
    goes way beyond reason.
That's Christmas!

And did you notice what happens in this inappropriate place
  with this unreasonable child?
Reconciliation takes place, something reason could never achieve,
  because it takes love.

This stable where he was born is
  a place that makes friends of all who gather here,
  a place of no jealousy,
  a place of the oldest Christian story of human joy,
  a place of hope,
  a place of love,
  and a place of faith.
That's Christmas!

Christmas is the feast of staying in touch:
  heaven in touch with earth.
  God in touch with people.
  Me in touch with you.

This reminds me of a cute story.
A little boy had just gotten his own room.
During his first night in it alone, a violent thunderstorm broke out.
The boy started screaming, "Daddy! Come quick! I'm scared!"

Don't worry, Bobby!" his father called out,
   "God loves you and will protect you."
The boy yelled back,
   "I know God loves me and will protect me.
   But right now I need somebody with skin on."
That's Christmas.

Num 6:22–27; Gal 4:4–7; Luke 2:16–21

A Time to Treasure

For many of us, the week between Christmas and New Year
    is filled not just with celebrations
        but also with information.
Magazines and newspapers are filled
    with flashbacks of the previous year and predictions for the next.
When we flip on the TV,
    we are confronted with the highlights of the past year,
    while the radio is playing the hits of the previous year.

Too much information can numb the mind and senses.
Even our daily diets are complicated with new information
    about nutritional values and health hazards.

It's the Information Age, but information alone does not enlighten.
Information may make us knowledgeable,
    but it does not necessarily make us wise.

There are millions of fragmented facts exploding around us,
    but the information alone is not an adequate guide to the future.

On this New Year's Day,
    the liturgy gives us an opportunity
        to go beyond the facts in the well-written story of Christ's birth.

As we celebrate the Solemnity of Mary,
    the liturgy gives us an opportunity to move with Mary
    and touch the deeper meanings of the nativity story.
In the gospel, we watch as the shepherds
    "went with haste and found Mary and Joseph,
    and the child lying in the manger.

When they saw this, they made known
    what had been told them about this child,
        and all who heard it were amazed." (Luke 2:16–18)

"But Mary treasured all these words
    and pondered them in her heart." (Luke 2:19)
Mary moves beyond the information and excitement of Christ's birth
    to be at one in the solitude of his presence.

These days after Christmas,
    let us, too, seek solitude,
    unafraid to be alone with our thoughts,
    with ourselves,
    and with God.

Like Mary, let us reflect on the activities of our daily lives
    to find meaning and a sense of worth in them.
Let us treasure the ordinary things
    and ponder them in our hearts.

When psychologist Eric Fromm was asked
    to give a simple recipe for psychic health, he replied:
"A half hour a day of solitude,
    or twice a day if you can afford it,
        will do wonders for your health."

So here is a New Year's resolution for you.
    Resolve to set aside a half hour of solitude a day—or two if you can afford it.

True solitude keeps us in touch with God
    and convinces us that ordinary things
    are precious, and sacred, and enough.

May this year be the year we find time for solitude and enlightenment.
May this be the year when we learn
    to treasure the simple things of life
        and "ponder them in our hearts."

1 Sam 1–20, 22, 24–28; 1 Jn 3:1–2, 21–24; Luke 2:41–52

Jesus, the Teenager

"Why were you searching for me?
Did you not know that I must be in my Father's house?" (Luke 2:49)

"Child, why have you treated us like this?
Look, your father and I
    have been searching for you in great anxiety,"
    his mother said. (Luke 2:48)

She could have said,
"We were frantic,
    we imagined muggings or kidnappings."

And Jesus was distressed
    at their distress,
        but he was still in another world,
        a world he had thought they would know about.

It was all so obvious to him…
If they loved him, it surely should be obvious to them too.

Jesus was saying, "I had to be here,
    in this house,
    in this place which is the heart of wisdom,
    the place of my Father.

As the story is written,
    the family was on the great yearly pilgrimage to Jerusalem,
        but this time Jesus was not a child.
He was Bar Mitzvah.
He was a "Son of the Law."

Jesus was once more in the holy city,
    with a new freedom to find his way,
        to pursue his questions.

But of course, loving them,
    he went home with them that day.
He fitted himself back into the familiar pattern,
    only the pattern had changed forever.
The Gospel of Luke wants to make this transition for Jesus clear for us.

When a child on the brink of adulthood
    breaks into a world beyond
        what his or her parents have known or seemed to know,
        it is hard for the parents.
It may be through an experience like going away to camp,
    or it may be through a volunteer experience,
    or through the arts, school, church, new friends.
Suddenly there is a gap between parent and child.

"They don't understand," is the teen's lament.
They, who had once seemed so wise,
    seem now too old, too worldly, too cautious.

And to the parents, the fledgling adult seems
    too impatient, not realistic, inconsiderate,
    ungrateful for all the care and protection
    that now seems to him or her like prison bars.

"Wait," say the parents.
"I can't wait," says the adolescent.
"You don't know," say the parents.
"I know," says the one who feels no longer a child.

One father tells the story
   of having lost his little four-year-old daughter for over an hour.
And when he found her playing at a neighbor's house, he asked,
"Why did you do this, Jolene?
I was worried and I didn't know where you were."
Jolene answered, "It's okay, Daddy, I knew where I was."

For parents, there is often a crisis,
   or more often a series of crises,
   sometimes small, sometimes big.
Each crisis is perhaps a dangerous time,
   but it is also a moment of new life for all involved.

On this Feast of the Holy Family,
Mary becomes for us the inspiration of a deep and persevering trust
   for all who do not fully understand,
      but are willing to grow in faith.
Together, with Joseph, she endures all the feelings
   involved in raising a child:
      astonishment, anxiety, amazement,
      lack of understanding, and love.

We can only wonder
   what the mixture of pain and joy was for Mary and Joseph,
      as they traveled back to Nazareth
      and took up the everyday tasks with a young man
      who would never be their child again.
We can only wonder how, in the months and years ahead,
   the family found new ways within their old ways.

There are signs enough in the other gospel stories
   that the relationship was not easy,
      and that is powerful encouragement to parents:
   Children are not your possessions
      but rather your companions on the pilgrimage of life.

And parents have to discover in themselves the wisdom of God
    to discern, to believe, to uphold, to restrain, to let go,
        and to recognize their mistakes.

Toward the end of this gospel passage,
    we read that Mary "treasured all these things in her heart" (Luke 2:51),
    until she grew to understand and accept the mission of her son.

The gospel passage concludes with the words,
"Then he went down with them and came to Nazareth,
    and was obedient to them." (Luke 2:51)
And he, "increased in wisdom and in years,
    and in divine and human favor." (Luke 2:52)

We are left with the reassuring thought
    that when family life is a mutually respectful affair
        between parents and children,
        both grow to full maturity.

At times it will be the children
    who do not understand their parents' concerns.
And sometimes it will be the parents
    who do not understand their children's need to separate themselves
    and extend their boundaries beyond the safety of a protective home.

But when both exercise trust and faith,
    both will, "increase in wisdom and years,
        and in divine and human favor." (Luke 2:52)

Today on this feast,
    let us celebrate the gift of family,
        the foundation of our society.

Let us ask God to bless our families
    with the spirit of loving trust and faith in each other,
especially those families
    who are going through some difficult times with their teenagers.
May they find joy and support in one another and also from us.

Isa 60:1–6; Eph 3:2–3a, 5–6; Mt 2:1–12

Becoming Magi

"A multitude of camels shall cover you,
    the young camels of Midian and Ephah:
    all those from Sheba shall come...." (Isa 60:6)

"Wise men from the East came to Jerusalem
    asking, 'Where is the child
        who has been born king of the Jews?'" (Matt 2:1)

"May the kings of Tarshish and of the isles
    render him tribute." (Ps 72:10)

Few New Testament stories have captured our imaginations
    like that of the Magi.
Indeed our imaginations have enlarged on this gospel story of Matthew.
We have decided that there were
    three Magi; we have made them kings,
        we have given them camels,
        and we've even assigned them names:
    Gaspar, Melchior, and Balthazar.

The very charm of the ancient story, however,
    may cause us to miss the point
        Matthew was trying to make in telling it.
He highlighted the contrast between the Jewish and Gentile reaction
    to the birth of the Messiah.

The Magi, who were not Jews, studied the stars,
    saw God's message, and traveled from afar
        to worship the newborn king.

The Jewish leaders, a few miles from Bethlehem,
    with Scriptures to guide them,
        knew exactly where Jesus would be born.
Yet, they failed to act on their knowledge
    other than to tell Herod, who sent soldiers to kill the child.

Matthew's point was that Jesus belongs to the world
    and not just to the Jewish people.
At the time this gospel was written (around 85 CE),
    the young Christian community had burst out of Palestine
        and entered the great world of the Roman Empire.
Gentile converts were entering the fold in growing numbers.
The early Church had determined that those new converts
    did not have to convert to Judaism in order to be Christian.

Making this decision, they followed the example of Jesus
    who rejected boundaries
        and welcomed everyone who came to him,
    pious and publican
    saint and sinner.

The solemnity of the Epiphany teaches us
    that we must be open and welcoming to others
        whatever their race, ethnic background,
        culture, gender,
        sexual orientation,
        or social class and standing.

It teaches us that God does not recognize these
    boundaries and borders,
        nor should those who gather around his Son
    in the community we call the Church.

He was a gift for all humankind,
    and the gifts of gold, frankincense, and myrrh
    were gifts in response.

But if Jesus came for all,
    he came only for those who search,
    for those who persist,
    for those who will not quit or give up,
    for those who will seek him out,
        no matter how weary, discouraged,
        or frustrated they may feel.

The search for Jesus is something like a treasure hunt.
We must find our way to Bethlehem,
    and it is a troubling and sometimes difficult journey.
We will never get there if we give up.

We will probably only find him completely and totally
    at the end of our life.
However, the more we search,
    we realize that the God revealed to us
        through the child of Bethlehem
        becomes the God for whom we seek.

All of us are born
    explorers, adventurers, romantics, and seekers.

We need to become once again like the Magi,
    people who would take the risk of crossing deserts
    because a star shone over a newborn babe.

We should seek the Babe of Bethlehem
    to stir us out of the routine and monotony of the winter months,
    to turn us
        from plodders to searchers of faith,
        from dullards to adventurers in our quest for meaning,
        from cynics to romantics in love with one another,
        from hardened realists
            to men and women of dreams and missions.

Like the Magi of old,
    let us make a deliberate decision to travel by another road.

All through our lives, let us be witnesses
    of the star we carry in our hearts.
May it be a light for all.

A Glimpse of Fr. Hayes

My family grew up in Duluth, Minnesota, and we were members of St. Michael's Catholic Church in Lakeside. We had the pleasure of having "young" Fr. Michael Hayes as our associate pastor. I will always remember him for his kindness, especially to my brother Bill.

Bill has a long history of drug and alcohol abuse. He struggles with these addictions on a daily basis. At one of his lowest points he turned to God and met Fr. Michael Hayes.

Fr. Mike would meet Bill for coffee and cigarettes at Bridgeman's, and they would talk for hours. They would walk the streets in Duluth and talk for hours. They would meet at church and talk for hours. Fr. Mike opened his home and his heart to Bill and gave him hope when Bill thought there was none. He was a friend when everyone else turned away. Fr. Mike helped Bill to find a reason to keep going.

Bill continues to struggle with these addictions, but the one constant in his life is his deep belief in God. He attends Mass on a regular basis, and I believe this is because of the kindness of Fr. Michael Hayes.

—Mary (Lyons) Johnson, Lakeville, MN

Isa 42:1–4, 6–7; Acts 10:34–38; Luke 3:15–16, 21–22

Another Epiphany

Like last Sunday, this one is an epiphany,
    a manifestation of Jesus as the Christ.
It is an epiphany of God in flesh and blood.

"You are my Son, the Beloved; with you I am well pleased." (Luke 3:22)

Last Sunday we read
    that the Magi found out who Jesus was…the Messiah.
Today, the gospel pushes us one step further.

Today, Jesus finds out who he is.

These Scriptures are about
    the radical, the new, the different.
Luke shapes this gospel so that we clearly see Jesus' baptism
    as the beginning of something new
        and radically different.

John preached a baptism of repentance, and forgiveness,
    and people responded.
But when Jesus went down into the water, it was not to be forgiven
    but to begin:
        to begin his proclamation of the kingdom,
        to begin his confrontation with the powers of death
        to begin the sending of the Holy Spirit
            into the lives of those who listened.

When Jesus went down into the water, it was not as a prophet, or a teacher,
    but as the Son, the Beloved One,
        the one who is God come among us.

The touching words of Isaiah help us realize
    that something new has happened.

"Every valley shall be lifted up,
    and every mountain and hill be made low;
    the uneven ground shall become level,
    and the rough places a plain." (Isa 40:4)

We are not to fear,
"Here is our God" (Isa 40:9),
    who has come with might and with tenderness.

"Speak tenderly to Jerusalem and cry to her
    that she has served her term
        that her penalty is paid." (Isa 40:2)

Billions of years ago, God began the work of creation.
The stars, the sun, the universe began,
    but our world, this act of creation,
        is not finished.

That's what today's feast of Jesus' baptism tells us.
God is not a distant or absent creator.
God has sent his Son among us.
God's Spirit is in the world,
    and the ways of the Spirit will be gentle.

Listen to Isaiah today:
"He will feed his flock like a shepherd;
    he will gather the lambs in his arms,
    and carry them in his bosom,
    and gently lead the mother sheep." (Isa 40:11)
Jesus' task is now our task and his ways should be our ways.

Today's feast reminds us who we are.
Martin Luther had many times of great doubt in his life,
    and he said that the only thing that kept him afloat
    was to touch his forehead, and repeat the words,
        "Baptismatus sum: I am baptized."

Our baptism is not just a baptism of water;
    it is a baptism of fire and spirit.
"He will baptize you with the Holy Spirit and fire." (Luke 3:16)

Fire as a symbol suggests love, a passionate, burning love,
    a love that burns away evil and warms the heart.

We are not only baptized but called to love as Jesus loved,
    or now, loves through us.

We are called to bring the fire of God's Spirit into the world,
    to change it and create in it.
"Come Holy Spirit, enkindle in us the fire of your love."

We are called by the Holy Spirit to listen to the Scriptures,
    not only with our mind
        but with our heart, as something we are to love and cherish.
Once in love with the Word of God,
    we are compelled to move and act with conviction.

The Bible has been compared to a cookbook.
What is a cookbook but a collection of recipes?
And what good are these if someone doesn't cook
    and really doesn't try out the recipes?
One doesn't keep cookbooks, of which some people have dozens,
    in the living room, but somewhere in the kitchen, ready to use.

We can keep the Bible wherever we wish,
    and read the Scriptures by ourselves,
        or discuss them in a group, study them in class,
        and come to church to hear the Word proclaimed.

But do we act upon what we hear?

Does it really change us?

Does it impel us to change our values?

Does it change the way we use time and money?

Does it make us resolve to be more compassionate people?

Does it challenge us to find ways to serve?

A recipe from a cookbook

or a gourmet magazine

can give us a good meal.

But the teaching of Jesus and the prophets can give us a good life

and reveal to us the purpose and meaning of life.

You just can't walk away from the Word of God.

The fire of God's Spirit

will give us an inner compulsion to do something.

In our Eucharist today,

let us pray that we will be true to our baptism;

that we be more open to God's action;

that we will be less afraid to die a little for the sake of Christ.

On this Feast of the Baptism of the Lord,

Let us renew our baptismal promises.

Remember that it is better to have made promises

and broken them,

than never to have promised at all.

Give yourself the gift of another Epiphany.

If you are willing to commit yourself anew

to our common task of building God's kingdom in our day,

I ask you to make this resounding response:

"Yes, I do believe!" to the following questions.

(The renewal of baptismal promises now follows.)

Lent & Easter

Joel 2:12–18; 2 Cor 5:20—6:2; Mt 6:1–6, 16–18

Burning Questions

The ashes placed on our foreheads this day
    are a kind of liturgical slap in the face to bring us to our senses.
We are signed with the cross as our first step towards Easter.
The cross of ashes is death and life in a single sign.

Ashes are the remains of something that has been burned.
Think about that, and what have we burned?
We use the word "burn" in any number of phrases or idioms.

For example,
we "burn our bridges."

In a very real sense that is what Lent is about.
We are burning the bridges between a former way of life
    and a new way of life.
The ashes remind us that we cannot go back to the way we were.

"We burn with passion."

This should be particularly true of us this Lent.
We must burn with the passion of our Lord Jesus Christ
    who suffered, died, and rose again for our salvation.
And we burn because we share the same passion, death and resurrection.

We "get burned."

This occurs when we find ourselves
    on the receiving end of a scam or a joke.
This will happen to us this Lent as well.
In fact, we need to get burned.

We have not always been good stewards of time, treasure, and talent.
We have played around with God's creation.
It's time to get pulled up short.
It's time we got burned.

"I'm burning with desire."
Again, this should be true of us this Lent.
The desire burning our spirits should warm us
    throughout this season
        as we strive to imitate the burning desire of Christ.

"I'm burned up."
This is what we say when people or circumstances take us to the edge.
We can't stand it any longer, whatever it is that challenges us.
Again, during this Lent, there are any number of things
    that should get us "burned up."

If we want ashes, so the physical sciences tell us,
    we have to burn material things.
But we know better.
There are spiritual ashes we need to create this Lent.
There are "burning questions" we need to answer
    about ourselves, our world, our God.
When we answer them,
    the ashes will make a fine decoration upon our heads.

What burning questions confront you this Lent as you take on these ashes?
    Are you trying to do for yourself what God wants to do for you?

Most of us are, you know.
We think we can get by on our own.
We reserve God for only special occasions,
    but we need God all the time.
So, one of our burning questions this Lent might be,
    "Who is God for me?"

Maybe you've answered that question.
You have not finished yet.
You have a further burning question,
     "How much do I want God to be there for me?"

Since we are material beings,
     we have only so much time and space at our disposal.
If all that time and space is filled,
     we have to start emptying things out:
          burn our bridges,
          burn with passion,
          get burned,
          burn with desire,
          be burned up,
          wrestle with the burning questions.

If we just do it, God guarantees that the fire will burn forever.
Our dusty creation is not the whole truth about human beings,
     just as the whole truth about Jesus is not only
          that he was separated from God.
A more complete picture will be revealed to us over the coming weeks,
     during the springtime of the Church.

And now we begin…
Come, receive the ashes of a forgotten fire.

Deut 26:4–10; Rom 10:8–13; Luke 4:1–13

The Desert

In all my years, one thing does not change.
However you disguise it, this thing does not change:
 the perpetual struggle of Good and Evil.

Second, you neglect and belittle the desert.
The desert is not remote in the southern tropics.
The desert is not only around the corner,
The desert is squeezed in the tube-train next to you.
The desert is in the heart of your brother.
—T.S. Eliot, "The Rock"

The unifying image of today's liturgy is the desert.
Our first reading outlines the ritual enjoined upon the Jewish people:
 this is the manner in which they will give thanks to God
  for their deliverance from Egypt.

But that deliverance was not accomplished
 without the desert experience.

The forty days Jesus spent in the desert
 echoes the forty years his ancestors wandered in the wilderness.
Our forty days of Lent are, of course, synonymous
 with the forty days Jesus spent in the desert.

Lent is the Church's desert.
It's a place of preparation and testing,
 a time for taking stock and repentance.

Unless we identify our emptiness,
 we will not recognize our need for God's fullness.

The desert is a place of temptation and terror.
It is a place of great loneliness and testing.

The desert cannot be avoided.
It can be kept at bay for a time perhaps,
    but the dark desert is as much part of us as our right hand.

The wastelands are within.
We neglect and belittle the desert at our peril.
We can resort to short-term expedients,
    to still the beasts that roam within.
We can anesthetize them, dupe them,
    or distract ourselves from them.

Luke tells us that Jesus was offered such short term solutions.

First he considered becoming an Economic Messiah.
It is easy to understand why he was hungry.
His own hunger reminded him of hungry people all over the world.
They would follow anyone who would feed them.
Jesus thought about doing that. It was his kind of thing.
He could not understand why some people had too much food
    while others did not have any.
That situation troubled him deeply,
    and he thought about devoting his life to the injustice.

Jesus answered the devil. Scripture has it,
    "One does not live by bread alone." (Luke 4:4)
Stones turned into bread before his eyes;
    he recognized this as a hollow promise.

The hunger of the human being runs much deeper,
    but it is not easy to dismiss this temptation.
We all like to make a contribution that is tangible, obvious, and visible.

Henri Nouwen is wise to remind us,
"The greatest paradox of our times
    is that many of us are busy and bored at the same time."
The question that must guide all organizing activity in a parish,
    is not how to keep people busy,
      but how to keep them from becoming so busy
        that they can no longer hear the voice of God
        who speaks in silence.
Jesus is not stating that bread is unnecessary;
    rather, he is stating that it is simply insufficient for all our needs.

"The last temptation is the greatest treason,
    to do the right thing for the wrong reason."
      So said T.S. Eliot in *Murder in the Cathedral*.

Having rejected the devil's empty charm
    of turning stones into loaves of bread,
      Jesus had the carrot of power dangled before him.
He also considered becoming a political messiah.

In what surely must be the closest biblical parallel to the satellite dish,
Luke tells us that the devil
    "showed him in an instant
    all the kingdoms of the world." (Luke 4:5)

He promised,
"To you I will give their glory and all this authority:
    for it has been given over to me, and I give it to anyone I please."
    (Luke 4:6)

The trappings of power have their attraction.
With Jesus' ability to lead and inspire,
    he could have built an army like none other.
He could have defeated Rome and conquered the world.
He could have used his position of power for good ends.
And he was tempted to do that.

Jesus stuck to his own vision of power as service:
"Worship the Lord your God and serve only him." (Luke 4:8)

Third, he thought about using his faith
    as an exemption from pain and suffering.
Since he was God's beloved Son, since divine favor rested upon him,
    surely he could expect special treatment.
The angels were in charge of protecting him.
He could leap from the top of the temple
    and they would save him from harm.

This is what faith means to some people.
You can hear it on TV each week.
If you trust God the right way,
    he will protect you and provide for your every need.

But Jesus rejected that way
    and chose to take the hard road with you and me.
The servant is not greater than his master.

We will all inevitably be forced one day into our own personal desert:
    whether through illness, unemployment, depression,
    broken relationships, compulsion, or betrayal.

We will be called upon one day to wrestle with one of these wild beasts.

We are called not to be brilliant, but to be faithful.
We are called not to be spectacular, but to be humble.
We are called not to be successful, but to be servants.

This is our vocation in time of temptation.

It was not easy for Jesus to resist,
    and we cannot believe it will be easy for us.
The only certainty
    is that Jesus understands and acknowledges our difficulty.
And he promises the guidance and strength of the Holy Spirit,
    this Lent and every day of our lives,
        to face temptation openly and honestly.

The liturgy of the First Sunday of Lent offers us hope
that if we have the strength to confront our temptations
with the eyes of faith, and reject short-term solutions,
we will emerge from our forty days in the desert
ready to greet the Easter dawn.

Our lenten prayer, fasting, and the sharing of charity
can be like the appetizers that make us hungry for the Easter feast.

Gen 15:5–12, 17–18; Phil 3:17—4:1 or 3:20–4:1; Luke 9:28b–36

I've Been to the Mountaintop

"I've been to the mountain (top)," he said on that day
   in front of the Lincoln Memorial in Washington, D.C.
And in that resounding, long ago speech,
   Dr. Martin Luther King, Jr., challenged and inspired the nation
      with his dream of a society
         without barriers of color, race, religion, or national origin.

Yes, he had been to the mountain, the place of inspiration.
People knew what he meant.
He had been to the mountaintop of his own spiritual enlightenment.
Yes, he had been led there by Jesus,
   and he had listened to his voice.

Then, as he spoke to those thousands in Washington,
   and indeed to the whole nation,
   he was in the valley,
      sharing the vision and leading the people
      to take one more step on the road to justice.

In the gospel lesson for today,
   the times were perilous for Jesus.
Jesus always began his preparation for a difficult journey
   with a focused time of prayer.
In fact, he started every great adventure with a prayer, a retreat.
   He was simply too busy not to pray.
He knew, as C.S. Lewis observed,
   "If the devil can't make you bad, he will make you busy."

Jesus took Peter, James, and John up the mountain
    because he wanted to pray.
Luke's gospel does not tell us that the disciples prayed, just Jesus.
They needed rest from their climb and from their labors in the valley below.

Jesus was tired too, but he needed something more than rest.
He had brought them half way to heaven,
    not for the view of the valley but the view of the sky.
And while they rested, heaven descended upon Jesus.
What dazzled the disciples was sheer glory!

Jesus climbed that hill to rest in the awareness
    that he was beloved of God
        and that his mission mattered to God.

It is very important to realize where Peter was at that moment.
Peter opted for piety.
"Master, it is good for us to be here; let us make three dwellings." (Luke 9:33)

After all, Peter knew a good thing when he saw it,
    and Peter planned to settle down there.
Peter decided that the spiritual has something to do with building temples.
Ah, yes, if there is a temptation in Christian ministry today,
    it is probably the temptation to play Church.

No sooner had Peter decided to be
    a church bureaucrat,
    a weekday mystic,
    and an office manager,
        look what happened.
Scripture tosses the entire thought into mid-air.
While he was still speaking, the voice of God said,
    "This is my Son, my Chosen; listen to him!" (Luke 9:35)

Suddenly Jesus was alone.
The Scriptures tell us that the disciples remained silent
    and told no one about what they had seen.

Then, slowly but surely, Jesus began to lead them
    around the edges of the cliffs, over the rocky road,
        and back down the mountain,
        to the very bottom of the hill,
        to the dirty town, and suffering people,
        and unbelieving officials, and ineffective institutions below.

We use the biblical image when we say of a high spiritual moment
    that it was a "mountaintop" experience.
But we also know that we do not stay up on those spiritual highs.
That would be too rarified an existence.
We descend to the valleys because that is where we live—
    emotionally, mentally, and spiritually.

Yet we find ourselves hoping once again to ascend the heights
    and renew our spiritual lives.
In a sense, that is why we come here,
    to listen again to Jesus,
    and let him teach and lead us in the days that lie before us.
We could have a "mountaintop" experience right here.

But we have to reflect on what happened
    after the vision on the mountaintop.
Do you remember that the disciples fell silent
    as Jesus led them down the trail once again to the valley?

Nothing left of the vision,
    no monument, no cairn of stones piled up.
Only the memory of three men who had been told to listen.

When Jesus and the disciples descended the mountain,
    they were met by a multitude of people, the spiritually needy.
And suddenly that need was focused on the person of a man
    who cried out to Jesus to heal his son.

We began with a follower of Jesus named Martin Luther King, Jr.,
    whose mountaintop experience inspired a ministry
        and a movement that helped to change a whole nation.

Our own inspirations may not be so impressive or visionary
    as were those of Peter, James and John,
        and of brother Martin, or others we could name.
But all we are asked to do is to serve where we are
    and in ways that we are able.

Remember the words,
    "This my Son, my Chosen, listen to him."
He is always with us and shows us the way.

On our lenten journey, we are asked to transfigure ourselves and each other
    by the power of God's love in us.
Our challenge is to remain with Christ on whatever hill,
    or in whatever valley we find him.

The baggage area is filled with people in expectation of an incoming flight.
After the plane lands and taxies slowly to the terminal,
    the travelers disembark
    and make their way through the tunneled walkway
    and down through security.
They are met by a sea of expressionless faces with searching eyes,
    darting from one passenger to another,
    looking for the welcome of a familiar face.
Then comes the moment of recognition.
    Eyes come alive and faces are transformed
    by the power of mutual love.

The transformation of mutual love
    is what we are about this lenten season.

A Glimpse of Fr. Hayes

I came into the rectory one day all excited because a wonderful thing had happened that was just a miracle as far as I was concerned. I excitedly told Fr. Mike about it, and as he sat in his recliner smoking a cigarette, he calmly said, "What a coincidence," or that's what I thought he said. I promptly replied, "I don't believe it was a coincidence. I know it was a miracle." He quietly said, "That's what I said; it is a co-incident with God." It was a humbling lesson for me.

—Janice Kilgore, Youth and Prison Minister
Holy Angels Church, Moose Lake, MN

Ex 3:1–8a, 13–15; 1 Cor 10:1–6, 10–12; Luke 13:1–9

The Second-Chance Gospel

I try to visualize the scene that aroused Moses' curiosity:
    an angel of the Lord in a bush that was aflame
    but not burning.
If something like this were to happen in one of our state or national parks,
    throngs of people would appear overnight to ooh and aah.
They would probably suggest that a shrine be built on the site.
The physicist would have
    some natural explanation for the occurrence,
        while the investor would be dreaming of how
        to commercialize the area and make big bucks.

Poor Moses was there alone.
    No one to ooh and aah with him except his sheep.
The humble shepherd just stood in awe
    and listened to what God was saying to him.

What is God saying to us in the parable of the fig tree, and what do we hear?

The message is:
    This is the gospel of the second chance.

It is a statement about God's patience, and a challenge to us
    to give others a second chance in a patient and hopeful way.

A writer tells this story.
    A rather famous painting shows a young man playing chess with the devil.
    They are playing for possession of the young man's soul.
    The painting portrays the devil as having made a brilliant move.
    Brendan Behan, an Irish writer, would say,
        "O! That filthy devil should stay below in hell."

Chess players who study the arrangement of the chess pieces in the painting
  feel immediate sympathy for the young man,
    for he has been put in a hopeless situation.
He has been led down a blind alley with no exit.

Pat Murphy, a former world class chess player,
  became intrigued by the painting.
One day while studying the arrangement of the chess pieces,
  he saw something that no one else did.
Excitedly,
  he cried out to the young man in the painting.

"Don't give up.
  You still have an excellent move left.
  There's still hope!"

The story fits in beautifully with the point that Jesus makes
  in the parable of the fig tree in today's gospel.
  Like the young man in the painting,
  the fig tree seems hopelessly lost.
  It is about to be cut down.
  Then suddenly a ray of hope breaks through.

There is a last minute reprieve, a last minute second chance!

The story of the young man and the parable of the fig tree
  contain an important message for us.
Because of Jesus
  we are never doomed.
No matter how bad things seem, there is hope for us.
No matter what situation we find ourselves in,
  because of Jesus
    there is always one more move to make,
    no matter how late in the game it is.

How does all of this apply to our lives in a practical way?
All of us, to some extent, are like the young man and the fig tree.

All of us, at one time or another,
    have arrived at a point in life
        when it seemed that we were in a no-win situation.
Perhaps some of us are at such a point right now in our lives.
Perhaps some situation threatens to overwhelm us.
Perhaps a certain problem has led us down a blind alley
    that seems to be a dead end.

It is right here that today's gospel has an important message for us.
Because of Jesus
    hope still remains for us, no matter what the situation.

This is the good news that we celebrate in today's liturgy.
This is the message that God wants us to carry back to the world this week.

Let us close with a poem.
It's about an old violin which, like us, was given a second chance.
It's yet another image of your story
    and my story
        and God's love for us.

I hope the poem will touch your hearts
    and move you to celebrate today's Eucharist
        with more than ordinary gratitude and love.

    It was battered and scarred and the auctioneer
    Thought it scarcely worth his while.
    To waste much time on the old violin.
    But he held it up with a smile.
    'What am I bid, good folk?' he cried.
    'Who'll start the bidding for me?
    A dollar, a dollar, then two, only two?
    Two dollars and who'll make it three?'

'Three dollars once and three dollars twice,
And going for three, but no!'
From the room far back a gray-haired man
Came forward and picked up the bow.
And wiping the dust from the old violin
And tightening the loosened strings,
He played a melody pure and sweet,
Sweet as an angel sings.

"The music ceased and the auctioneer
In a voice that was quiet and low
Said, 'What am I bid for the old violin?'
And he held it up with the bow.
'A thousand dollars and who'll make it two?
Two thousand and who'll make it three?
Three thousand once, three thousand twice
And going and gone!' said he.

The people cheered, but some of them cried,
'We don't quite understand.
What changed its worth?' Quick came the reply:
'The touch of the Master's hand.'
And many a man with life out of tune
And battered and scarred with sin
Is auctioned cheap to the thoughtless crowd,
Much like the old violin.

A mess of pottage, a glass of wine,
A game and he travels on.
He's going once, he's going twice,
He going and almost gone.
But the Master comes and the foolish crowd
Never can quite understand
The worth of the soul and the change
That's wrought
By the touch of the Master's hand.

—Myra Brooks Welch

Josh 5:9a, 10–12; 2 Cor 5:17–21; Luke 15:1–3, 11–32

It Happens Every Sunday

"And at the end of all our exploring
    will be to arrive where we started
    and know the place for the first time."
—T.S. Eliot

The Story of the Prodigal Son, or retitled
    the Story of the Forgiving Father, is like all parables.
Its structure is simple.
Its characters are few,
    and it lacks a conclusion.
Because of this, it is up to us to supply the ending today.

We ask, "What does it mean?"
    when we should be asking, "What can it mean?"

What about that older brother? How will this script end?

Charles Dickens calls this parable "the most touching story in literature."

The details of the younger son's behavior are not the point of the story.
His sin was not so much what he had done, but where he was.
Jesus called it "a distant land."
That describes, not his geographical location,
    but his "spiritual condition."

The wayward son had separated himself
    from the place to which he truly belonged.
When the boy got close to home,
    he discovered that someone
        was looking and longing and running to meet him.

The speech he had planned "Father, I have sinned" (Luke 15:21),
   was smothered in the embrace of his waiting father.

This would have been a good place for Jesus to have stopped the story!
   Right at that point the people were nodding in approval,
      but Jesus did not stop there.
He went on to point out that there is more than one kind of sin
   and more than one kind of sinner.

There are the sins of the far country
   and the sins of the father's house.
There are sins of the flesh
   and sins of the spirit.
There are sins of passion
   and sins of disposition and attitude.

Jesus said of the elder son,
   "Then he became angry and refused to go in." (Luke 15:28)

That is his disposition, his attitude or, as it is said today,
   "He had an attitude."
He was obviously selfish.
It did not matter if his attitude spoiled the party.
He just wanted to be sure that everybody knew
   how badly he had been treated.

This fellow looks strangely familiar to me.
I have seen him at family celebrations many times.
Worse yet, I have caught glimpses of him inside myself.
All of us, at least at times, are like the silly and selfish older brother.
   His refusal to forgive may have fractured the family
      far more than what the younger son had done.

No doubt the father was initially hurt and harmed
   by the younger son's actions in leaving, and perhaps he was angry.
But the father had managed to forgive.
It probably was not a clear-cut, one-time decision.

Forgiveness usually takes time.

It cannot be forced.
We have to acknowledge the anger and hurt that is there.
We need to heal the wounds before we can truly forgive,
    and we can't rush the healing process.

By the time the younger son came to his senses,
    the loving father had already been healed of his hurt.

The elder son had not yet begun the process of forgiveness.
    "He became angry and refused to go in." (Luke 15:28)
He was disturbed by what had transpired.
We get the impression that he would remain distressed and angry
    until he took the time and made the effort
        to heal the hurt he was experiencing.

The important lesson is
    that forgiveness doesn't happen all of a sudden like a miracle.
It takes time.

Anger is a very human emotion. Even Jesus got angry.
It is quite normal to feel angry towards someone who has hurt us.
    But we need not spend the rest of our lives
      hurting and hiding and hating
      because of something that happened in the past.

It is not a question of being totally forgiving
    or totally angry with someone.

It takes time to fully appreciate how we have been hurt by someone.
Slowly and surely, we can unclench our fists a little
    while we increase in forgiveness.

Terry Anderson, an American journalist
    held captive in Lebanon in the late 1980s,
    was able to forgive the people who held him captive
    because he thought about it, prayed about it,
    and gradually grew in forgiveness during his 2,455 days of captivity.

As a result, upon his release he was able to say,
"I'm a Christian and a Catholic.
It is required of me that I forgive, no matter how hard it may be."

If he had not forgiven them, he would have remained a captive,
    if not physically, certainly emotionally and spiritually.

Inner peace is found by changing ourselves,
    not changing the people who hurt us.

Forgiveness grew gradually for Terry Anderson,
    and for the loving father, and in any other person
        who has experienced pain from the actions and words of another.

Let us take heart from today's gospel story.
It reminds us that we are welcome at God's table in our incompleteness.
We don't need to have everything resolved before approaching this table,
    and that is probably why many of us are here today.
None of us is perfect or has it all together.
We still have much to figure out, and we are not always completely reliable.

But the music has begun.
The band has started to play.
And we are invited to celebrate and rejoice,
    whether we are wayward or reconcilers,
        for we are both.

It happens every Sunday.

Isa 43:16–21; Phil 3:8–14; John 8:1–11

Erasing Our Sins

"From the actions of humankind,
    it seems to me as if this particular planet of ours
        must be the insane asylum for some other world."
—George Bernard Shaw

From the beginning,
    people have been more than curious
    about what Jesus traced on the sand.

St. Jerome was one of the first serious speculators.
He guessed that when Jesus bent down,
    he traced the sins of those men
        seeking to stone the woman to death.

Some have suggested a spiritual reason.
Jesus' tracing was a silent time to pray
    to the Father for advice.

Others have offered more practical reasons.
Jesus was simply doodling in the sand
    until the time was right to speak,
    or even waiting for the lover's partner,
        the man to be dragged before the crowd of accusers.
Strict observance of the Mosaic law demanded this.
And on and on the speculation continues about what he wrote.

I suggest that maybe Jesus was not tracing but erasing.

This theory would make sense in light of the first reading
    from the prophet Isaiah.

The Babylonian exile is at an end,
   and the history of the earlier deliverance from Egypt is recalled.
God's mighty deeds had freed their ancestors.

But the poet then abruptly breaks off from his reminiscing:
"Do not remember the former things,
   or consider the things of old." (Isa 43:18)

He appeals to his people to forget the past, and to look to the future.
   "I am about to do a new thing." (Isa 43:19)

People who have suffered greatly have two options:
   either to wallow in past misery, to pick over the carcasses of injustice,
      or take up the reins again and begin life anew.
Prisoners of the past have no future.
Sinners who are obsessed with the past
   will fail to see the new things God is doing.

What is jolting about this reading is that
   God tells the people to "cut it out"!
Remember not the events of the past;
   the things of long ago consider not.

In other words,
   forget the "good old days" when God was on their side.
As Bob Dylan wrote,
   "For you never ask questions when God's on your side."

And then the Lord says,
   "I am about to do a new thing." (Isa 43:19)

So when Jesus bent down,
   he may have been erasing in the sand,
      not just the sins of those present,
      but all their past glories as well!

Jesus may have been erasing
    all those patriarchal interpretations of religious and social life
    that kept women "in their place."
Jesus bent down and erases in the sand
    not just their sins
        but the narrow interpretations they still cling to.

In Rome recently there was a four-day meeting
    between thirty-four American archbishops and Vatican officials.

One of their topics was divorce.
Fingers were pointed at the American church
    for granting too many annulments.
Some Vatican officials criticized the ease in obtaining annulments
    and that women religious were employed in diocesan marriage tribunals.

One cardinal declared,
"Women religious can be very helpful in dealing with marriage cases,
    but we have to be careful that their tender hearts
        do not play tricks on them."

We can only pray that the Church, too,
    will pay attention to Jesus erasing in the sand,
        not just people's sins
        but the tired old memories and interpretations
        some persons still cling to.

"Just for Men."
What the Church needs now is
    not to cling to the male domination of the past
    but to pay attention
        to the tender and tough hearts of women so long ignored.

What the Church needs now is
    not to cling to the good old days of power
    when the Church spoke, and the people jumped.

But the Church needs to listen
to the struggles and joys of ordinary people today,
and then speak against sin with Jesus' voice of compassion.

The story of the woman taken in adultery
does not appear in the gospel of John until the third or fourth century.
It seems that the reason this story took so long to be included in the Bible
is that during that period church authorities
were trying to enforce a strict discipline over marriage.
The story of the woman caught in adultery
seemed at that time to encourage laxity in marriage standards.

St. Augustine said that some were afraid
the gospel passage would give women an excuse to sin.
I'm not sure why their concern focused on women.
Obviously, there was a man involved,
and he got off scot-free.
He wasn't even subjected to public scorn.
So, if the story would give women an excuse to sin,
why not men?

Hopefully, we have gone beyond this kind of thinking,
especially the sexism of it.
But we are still troubled by this story.
It just isn't tough enough on crime.
We are opposed to mercy
for fear that it will reveal that we are "soft on crime"!

Jesus did not even threaten the woman, let alone punish her.
He simply said, "Neither do I condemn you.
Go your way, and from now on do not sin again." (John 8:11)

This woman must have thought her life was ruined forever.

But she left there that day with a second chance.
It was purely a matter of grace.
She did not earn any of it.

What could be more wonderful than that.
Yet the evidence suggests that we are sometimes troubled by it.

Why has the Church been so slow to embrace this story of grace?

On the appointed date, at the appointed time in Texas (1998),
murderess Karla Faye Tucker was put to death.
Was justice done? Only God knows.
We cannot help wondering.
There is no denial of criminal behavior,
    or underestimating the crime.

"Let anyone among you who is without sin
    be the first to throw a stone at her." (John 8:7)

The law prescribed one thing,
But grace provides another, and that may offend us.

Of this much I'm sure.
When we feel most justified in our actions
    is when we need to be most careful.
Check out the scribes and Pharisees in this story.

This world is not divided between saints and sinners,
    good people and bad people.
The grace of God puts us all on the same level.
The woman taken in adultery and her accusers were all sinners.

Karla Faye Tucker and her executioners,
    those who pled for her life, including the pope,
    and those who celebrated her death,
        were all sinners.
In the eyes of God we all stand on equal ground.

Maybe this is why grace sometimes offends us.
At this liturgy let us look on our sins,
    the stone in our hands,
    and the times when grace offended us,
        and seek forgiveness.

Thank God that this gospel survived.

"Woman where are they? Has no one condemned you?"
She said, "No one, sir."
And Jesus said, "Neither do I condemn you.
    Go your way, and from now on do not sin again." (John 8:11)

Jesus' gift to the woman was her life,
    a life made whole again
        by his compassionate justice.
For showing such mercy, Jesus would pay with his own life.

A Glimpse of Fr. Hayes

In one of our wedding preparation classes, Fr. Mike suggested that we have our session on the golf course. Since I had never played before, and Alvin, my fiancé, had played only a couple of times, we thought it would be "fun."

Well, it took the three of us all afternoon to play just nine holes. When we finished, Fr. Mike said to us, "If you can survive this afternoon on the golf course, you will have no problems in your marriage!" Needless to say, after fourteen years of marriage and two children, we are still very happily married. However, I have never played golf again.

—Courtney Johnson, former parishioner of St. Francis, Carlton, MN

Isa 50:4–7; Phil 2:6–11; Luke 22:14—23:56

The Entrance

"I don't know what I have said until I understand what you have heard."

The Passion speaks for itself.

Entrance seems to be the key
  to understanding the liturgy of Passion Sunday.
On this day the Church celebrates Christ's entrance into Jerusalem
  to accomplish his paschal mystery.

We enter into Jerusalem with Christ.
We enter into our holiest week.
We enter into our final preparation for the Easter feast.

I have just proclaimed the gospel account
  of Jesus' triumphant entrance into Jerusalem,
  and we go with Christ into Jerusalem.

We enter into the gospel.
  "The crowd that went ahead of him and who followed were shouting,
  'Hosanna to the Son of David'"

It was a joyful and triumphant procession!

However, once we have completed the procession
  we hear one of the "suffering servant" poems from Isaiah.

"I gave my back to those who struck me,
   and my cheeks to those who pulled out the beard;
I did not hide my face from insult and spitting.
The Lord God helps me; therefore I have not been disgraced;
   therefore I have set my face like flint,
   and I know that I shall not be put to shame." (Isa 50:6–7)

The second reading, the beautiful passage from the letter to the Philippians, summarizes the meaning of this holiest week.

"Christ Jesus who, though he was in the form of God,
   did not regard equality with God as something to be exploited,
but emptied himself, taking the form of a slave,
   being born in human likeness,
   And being found in human form,
he humbled himself and became obedient to the point of death—
   even death on a cross.

Therefore God also highly exalted him
   and gave him the name that is above every name." (Phil 2:5–9)

We are faced with the mystery of death and resurrection,
   loving service, and glorious exaltation.

The gospel proclaimed on this day is so central to the Passion
    that it gives its name to the whole day,
        Passion Sunday.

This year the gospel is from Luke.

The Passion is read, and we find ourselves going with Christ to Calvary
    and standing at the foot of the cross.
The Passion is dramatized with several readers
    to help make the story more alive and present to us.

The priest speaks the words of Jesus.
A second reader narrates
    and a third proclaims the words of the other persons
        in the gospel narrative.

You are invited to proclaim the words of the crowd,
    reminding all of us that it is indeed our story.

We find ourselves calling out,
    "Crucify him! Crucify him!"

Only a moment ago we were triumphantly singing,
    "Hosanna! Blessed is he who comes in the name of the Lord."

The contrast is so striking that I can forget
    that this is all too often the story of my life.
One moment
    I am full of good resolutions and promises to follow Christ.
And yet
    when the times get hard,
        I am among those who crucify Jesus by my sins.

By entering into the liturgies of Passion Sunday more reflectively
   and sharing in the Paschal Triduum,
   beginning with the Mass of the Lord's Supper and ending with Easter,
      we take the vital steps toward
         becoming better and more consistent disciples of Christ.
I urge you to go out of your way
   and attend the full reenactment of the events of our salvation.

We enter with the Savior into Jerusalem.
We meet him at the table where he becomes the Bread of Life for us.
We are moved by the Passion according to John,
   and we celebrate the Vigil Mass of Easter,
   the mother of all Masses.

Ex 12:1–8; 1 Cor 11:23–26; John 13:1–15

The Same Christ

Eucharist is Jesus crying out love with his life.
We are Eucharist,
    blessed, broken, and shared
        with one another.

There is an intimate connection between the Body of Christ,
    which is the Eucharist,
        and the Body of Christ,
which is the Community of Faith.
It is one and the same Christ,
    both in the Eucharist, and in the community;
        they are just different ways for the same Christ
to be present to us.

Showing deep reverence for the Body of Christ, the community,
    is the best way to show reverence for the Body of Christ, the Eucharist.
In fact, it is the best possible sign
    that we are receiving the Eucharist worthily.

I am not saying that other signs of reverence
    for the Eucharist are unimportant,
        but I am saying that the best and most important
            sign of reverence for Christ in the Eucharist
                is our reverence for Christ in the Community of Faith.
And, in fact, such reverence for Christ in the community
    is the best preparation for receiving Christ in the Eucharist.

The question then is this:
How do I show reverence for the body of Christ,
    the community of faith?

In the light of Christ, the answer is simple:
    by washing the feet of Christ in the community of faith;
    by washing each other's feet with humility and love
        as Jesus told us to do.

The husband and wife who defer to one another out of love,
    and who put up with each other's shortcomings out of love,
        are washing each other's feet,
    Christ's feet in the community.

Parents who attend to their children's needs
    and accept primary responsibility
    for their children's growth in faith, prayer, and holiness
        are washing their children's feet,
    Christ's feet in the community.

And older children who attend to the needs of their aged parents
    are washing their parent's feet,
    Christ's feet in the community.

Those who feed the hungry, clothe the naked,
    comfort the sick, visit the imprisoned, heal the broken-hearted,
        are washing the feet of the needy,
    Christ's feet in the community.
For what we do for the least among us, we do for Christ among us.

To wash each other's feet with love in these
    and a thousand other ways
        is to wash Christ's feet in the community.
This more than anything else prepares us to receive
    the Body of Christ in the Eucharist
        with sincere love and genuine reverence.

To say this in another way,
    to be without reverence for the community,
    and yet to think we can receive the Eucharist with reverence
        is a fundamental error of Christian living.

It divides Christ against himself,
  and I repeat,
    it is the same Christ both in the Eucharist
    and in the community of faith.

We cannot be in holy communion with the Lord in the Eucharist,
  if we are not in holy communion
    with the Lord in the community.

Let us, therefore, wash each other's feet out of love,
  as a sign of our communion with one another,
    knowing that we are washing the feet of Christ
  who first washed ours with his blood.

A Glimpse of Fr. Hayes

My cousin, Peg Flanagan, had a memorable first encounter with Fr. Mike. I was staying with her on a Sunday night so I could attend a graduate class in the morning. Fr. Mike decided to drive down from Moose Lake and meet Peg and take us to dinner.

He pulled up to the curb of her quaint Warwick Cottage in his rattletrap, smoke-filled car that served as his mobile office. We saw him trying to shuffle papers, books, and his venerable, beat-up briefcase to make room for us as we approached.

We were barely introduced when he started to fumble with a cassette tape in the dash of the car. He turned to Peg and said, "I want you to listen to this and see if it might work for a homily this weekend." On came the most twangy country and western tune: "You're So Heavenly-Minded, You're No Earthly Good."

After several libations at O'Connell's, Peg did indeed think it would work very well for the Sunday ahead. This was that homily.

Isa 52:13—53:12; Heb 4:14–16, 5:7–9; John 18:1—19:42

Is He Our King?

The major theme of John's gospel in chapters 18 and 19
    is the kingship of Christ.
Pilate ironically paid Jesus the highest tribute,
    placing on the cross an inscription written in three languages:
        "Jesus of Nazareth, the King of the Jews."
In the act of defiance directed at the chief priests,
    Pilate unwittingly extended the royalty of Jesus
        far beyond the borders of Judea.

John has woven into his telling of the trial and passion of Jesus
    a profound study of Pilate,
so we can take a close look at him
    and surprise, surprise!
As we do this, each one of us will find the royal claim of Jesus
    intruding into our conscience,
        the place where he really seeks enthronement.

What we know of Pilate can be quickly summed up.
He was the Roman Procurator from 26 to 36 CE.
The volatile Middle East was not an easy place to be assigned.
Keeping order required a strong hand, which he had.

Pilate spilled the blood of some Galilean zealots.
He provoked a public uproar and had to crack heads.
Like all Roman administrators,
    he was impatient with the religious practices and disputes
        in this part of the world.

It is also reported that he was finally recalled to Rome
    to answer for his mistaken slaughter of some Samaritans,
    and from there he just seems to disappear into history.

We do know that he was married
    and his wife Procula was with him in Jerusalem.
Matthew reports that she had a bad dream
    and warned him to do nothing to the innocent Jesus.

Suffice it to say that Pilate had a tough job
    in a complicated part of the world.
Given the way some of our leaders and appointees have blundered
    in various places on this globe,
    we can refrain from passing too harsh a judgment on Pilate.

In the gospels, Pilate is not presented as a brutish person.
John puts a rather human face on the man.

He really didn't want to get involved in a Jewish religious quarrel,
    or even in a criminal case that they could handle by their own laws.
When the captors of Jesus mentioned that they desired the death penalty,
    he had to interrogate Jesus.

"Are you the king of the Jews?" (John 18:33)
He had to have an answer to that question.
Jesus put him off balance,
"Do you ask this on your own,
    or did others tell you about me?" (John 18:34)

He confronted Pilate with the responsibility of making up his own mind. He
cleverly implied that Pilate might have some interest in him.
Hear Pilate's reply:
    "I am not a Jew, am I?" (John 18:35)

Unnerved,
    he still had to determine the reason why Jesus was handed over to him.
    "What have you done?" (John 18:35)

Jesus did not answer directly, but spoke of a kingdom not of this world.
   "So, you are a king?" (John 18:37)

Jesus reminded Pilate that he was the one who said that Jesus was a king.

Then Jesus stated his mission,
"For this I was born, and for this I came into the world,
   to testify to the truth.
Everyone who belongs to the truth listens to my voice." (John 18:37)

Pilate was rattled and asked the question,
   "What is truth?" (John 18:38)

Was this a cynical reply,
   or the beginning of interest,
   or simply a lack of comprehension?

At any rate, Pilate did not wait for an answer.
This portion of John's narrative ended with a question.
It was just left there dangling.

Maybe John wanted us to reflect on who or what truth is.

As the narrative moves on,
   you will recall how Pilate tried in one way or another to release Jesus.
Pilate resisted pressure until the enemies of Jesus
   played their trump card,
      reminding Pilate that Caesar would not want him
         to tolerate any other authority in Judea.

In the end, Pilate acted to save his own skin.
The pressure was too great and he resorted to expedience.
He had no central core of integrity, and so he compromised.

Søren Kierkegaard called the Word of God
   "a mirror in which we see our own reflection."

Well, here we are face to face with Pilate.
Or is that our own face staring back at us?

Did you know that Pilate is a saint in the Ethiopian church?
There is a tradition that he was a secret Christian.

We can doubt that,
    but there is no doubt that a lot of the people
        who read John's gospel
        were secret Christians within the establishment.
They feared public intimidation and so silenced their convictions.
Remember that Nicodemus came to Jesus in the night.

Many of those would see mirrored in Pilate
    their own tragic temporizing and indecision.

What about us?
I can't speak for you,
    but I know that on some issues,
    I have learned to tolerate a dull ache in the region of my conscience.

Pilate caved in when his own self-interest was at stake.
Do we do the same thing?
Suddenly now the focus is not on Pilate but on us.

This gospel brings the kingship of Christ to us
    with uncomfortable questions.
Where do we stand in terms of his royal claim upon us
    who bear his name?
Is he our King?

If so,
"Let every heart prepare him room
    for he is coming soon.
For us, there are still days of grace,
For we have yet to finish our race."

A Glimpse of Fr. Hayes

The Christian churches of Moose Lake had a remarkable relationship nourished by their pastors. During Holy Week they would have ecumenical services. Starting with Passion Sunday, the congregations would meet at Hope Lutheran Church, read the opening Scriptures, and with their pastors, they would then parade together through the streets with palm branches until they came to their own church for services. You need to remember that northern Minnesota weather wasn't always kind at that time of the year.

On Good Friday, one of the churches would host the others for an afternoon of Scripture and prayer. Fr. Hayes preached this homily for such an occasion as well as for the evening service at Holy Angels.

Acts 10:34a, 37–43; Col 3:1–4 or Cor 5:6b–8; John 20:1–9

Crunch, Munch, Munch, Munch

"Nothing worth proving can be proved, nor yet disapproved."
—Alfred Lord Tennyson

That is certainly true of Easter.
The resurrection of Christ is not something that can be proved
    like a mathematical formula.

Nietzsche once wrote, "Only where graves are, is there resurrection."

Easter is not just an historical event that happened one time, long ago.
Yet, we think of it in the past tense.
Easter is also a statement about you and me and our possibilities now.
Anytime we find the courage to rise above the past and live again,
    that is a little bit of Easter.

Each year the University of Chicago
    invites one of the greatest minds in theological education to give a lecture.
This one year the great Paul Tillich came to speak.

Dr. Tillich spoke for two and a half hours
    about how the historical resurrection was false.
He quoted scholar after scholar and book after book, concluding
    that since there was no such thing as the historical resurrection,
    the Christian tradition was groundless, emotional mumbo-jumbo
        because it was based on a relationship with a risen Christ
        who, in fact, never rose from the dead in any literal sense.
Then he said, "Are there any questions?"

After a deafening silence,
      a dark-skinned Southern preacher with woolly-white hair
      stood up in the back of the auditorium.

"Docta Tillich, I got a question," he said as all eyes turned toward him.
He reached into his bag lunch and pulled out an apple.
      "Docta Tillich"
            Crunch, Munch, Munch, Munch.
      "My question is a simple question."
            Crunch, Munch, Munch, Munch.
      "Now, I ain't ever read those books you read."
            Crunch, Munch, Munch, Munch.
      "And I can't recite the Scriptures in the original Greek.
            Crunch, Munch, Munch, Munch.
      "I don't know nothing about Niebuhr and Heidegger.
            Crunch, Munch, Munch, Munch.
      He finished his apple and began to lick his fingers
            "All I want to know is: This apple I just ate, was it bitter or sweet?"
Dr. Tillich answered in scholarly fashion:
      "I can't possibly answer your question for I haven't tasted your apple."

The white-haired preacher dropped the core of his apple into his paper bag,
      squeezed it and looked up at Dr. Tillich and said calmly,
            "Neither have you tasted my Jesus."

I love that story.

The Easter story is the story of a successful restoration to life after death,
      not by medical science but by God.

"Now the green blade rises from the buried grain,
Wheat that in the dark earth many days has lain;
Love lives again, that with the dead has been;
Love is come again
Like wheat that springs up green."
—John M. C. Crum

"Why do you look for the living among the dead?" (Luke 24:5)

We run the risk of placing Easter in the past.
Why do we look in the past for one who lives right now?
Maybe it's easier?
Maybe nobody has pointed out to us that we're looking in the wrong place.

The two men in dazzling garments said to them,
    "Why do you look for the living among the dead?"

But the men in brilliant clothes still call to us,
    still challenge us to open our eyes,
    to stop looking for the Living One among the dead.
So look around you this Easter night and seek the signs of the Living One.

In the Easter Proclamation we sing
    that "The power of this holy night dispels all evil,
    washes guilt away, brings mourners joy.
    It casts out hatred, brings us peace, and humbles earthly pride."

This is the power of the Risen One,
    and it is here and it is active.
Even in our battered and bruised and half-dead Church,
    the power of the Risen One is still here.

He still brings mourners joy.
He still casts out hatred.
In all our turmoil, he still brings peace.
That's the power of the One who is alive and alive now.

"Love lives again."

Acts 5:12–16; Rev 1:9–11a, 12–13, 17–19; John 20:19–31

Saint of the Second Opinion

This gospel is always a favorite because we recognize ourselves in Thomas.
He may be called Thomas the Twin,
  but he has passed into history as Thomas the Doubter.
It's a little unfair, isn't it?

After all, the gospel ends with that splendid profession of faith in five words,
  "My Lord, and my God!" (John 20:28)
And that was how the early Christians
  summed up their new-found faith/belief.
"Jesus is Lord."

There are two approaches to doubt and doubting.
One sees it as a lack of faith, even a sin.
Indeed, the older catechisms formally labeled it a sin to doubt revealed truth,
  to doubt what the Church teaches.

But change happens to us.
  As children, the faith was handed down to us,
  and we grew out of it after childhood.
"When I was a child, I spoke like a child,
  I thought like a child, I reasoned like a child;
    when I became an adult, I put an end to childish ways." (1 Cor 13:11)

But many haven't.
God for them may still be
  a policeman, a Santa Claus, an old man in the sky.

To doubt is to ask questions,
  or it should be that way, not a cynical withdrawal.

We examine what is passed on to us as truth
    and decide as adults if we really believe it,
    if we can ascend to it.

We look for evidence as Thomas did.
Thomas could be called the patron of those who want a second opinion.

Thomas heard those wonderful words from his friends,
    "We have seen the Lord!" (John 20:24)
He has the testimony of credible witnesses; he has their word for it.
But he wanted the evidence of his senses,
    to see with his own eyes, to touch with his own hands.
As it turns out, he doesn't touch the wounds or see with his own eyes,
    but simply responds to Jesus' voice.

Thomas comes out all the stronger for his doubting.
Consider a statement of faith that is often doubted or rejected,
    and see if we can come out like Thomas,
    all the stronger for our doubting.

Subject: The existence of God.
Why do people doubt the existence of God
    when the world itself—
    the cosmos, the universe,
    the earth, and all that exists—
    is an argument for a Creator?
The universe does not explain itself and how it came to be
    and why it is still becoming or evolving.

We have learned in our time
    how DNA works and how cells assume their function
      and life unfolds.

But why all this happens
    or where it has received this astonishing ability
      remains a mystery.

It is a mystery that many are willing to locate in God
　　but not all.

A famous scientist, Jacob Bronowski,
　　wrote a major book on science and culture called *The Ascent of Man*.
He describes in three short pages how the wheat plant evolved.

In the beginning there were only wild grasses
　　that wasted their seeds in the wind.
It was a kind of wild wheat but useless.

When it crossed with other plants and became a fertile hybrid,
　　he says that this happened
　　　"by some genetic accident."
When the plant crossed again, he explains it by saying,
　　"There was a second genetic accident."

The process of crossing and fertilizing it
　　resulted in a plant with forty-eight chromosomes,
　　and the heavy head of grain that we grind into flour and make bread.
He sums up the whole process by calling it
　　"a truly fairy tale of genetics."

For him,
　　accidents and fairy tales are the only explanation for a phenomenon
　　that resulted in a great advance in civilization.

At least he mentions in passing
　　the priest-scientist, Gregor Mendel,
　　who is called the father of genetics.
This is the same person
　　who matched peas so laboriously to discover their secret.

Mendel was obviously a believer.
So you take your choice.

If you believe it is all accidents and fairy tales that produced wheat,
    and our bodies, and millions of other bodies,
    then you don't need a Creator,
        a wisdom that precedes all things
            and is in all things.

We commonly refer to this wisdom as Creator, Spirit, or God.
Creation has rightly been called God's first Word.
It is a form of revelation, the first invitation to belief.
But it is not enough.

Nothing in nature will tell you
that you are loved, forgiven, cherished, or called to eternal life.
For that you need the Word made flesh,
    the One we know as Jesus, the Christ.

The doubts may vanish, but we never fully understand;
    we are dealing with the mystery of life, of God.

The Risen Lord was not so much impressed with Thomas
    as he is with us,
    who still struggle to believe.
He says of us,
"Blessed are they who have not seen,
    and yet have come to believe." (John 20:29)
Even now, that blessing is ours.

Yes, we are an Easter people and Alleluia is our song,
    but we are also a pilgrim people,
    not quite there and so we sing our Alleluia a little off-key.
With some hesitation we've heard the words,
    but have not always seen the signs.

May we not only look for signs of faith
    but learn to become such signs for one another
        throughout this Easter Season.

"Love is come again,
    like wheat that springs up green."

Maybe my vestments are not as brilliant
    as the clothes of the men in the tomb,
    but from this "man in white" this night
        hear a humble word of hope.

Look in the present and see the signs of love that come again,
    love that lives again.

Acts 5:2–14, 22–33; Rev 5:11–14; John 21:1–19 or 21:1–14

Joy

"Joy is the infallible sign of the presence of God."
—Georges Bernanos

"Come and have breakfast." (John 21:13)
Another translation says,
"Come, and eat your meal."

Surely this is the language of the Lord's supper,
    a eucharistic language,
        which turns up so often in the gospels.

We remember how, the night before he died,
    he presided at a meal
    and invited them for the first time
    to eat the bread
    that he broke as he said,
        "Take, eat; this is my body." (Matt 26:26)

We have never ceased to answer that invitation.
And when we gather
    in faith and love,
    obedient to his command,
        we are like those first disciples.
        We know it is the Lord.

Faith does not need to ask.
    Within ourselves we experience his presence.

There are many approaches to this beautiful gospel,
    take one that you like if it leads you to the Lord.

The Scriptures work like that,
    some more than others.

We are in the full light of Easter these seven weeks,
    when we should read and ponder
    each of the stories of the resurrection,
    all the encounters of the disciples with the risen Christ.

Think of them briefly.

On Easter morning he appeared first to Mary Magdalene
    whose love persevered after his death.
She returned to find the empty tomb and met him in the garden.

He appeared to the disciples in the upper room, and their dismay was ended,
    their fear turned to joy.

He appeared to the two disciples on the road to Emmaus
    in the most richly symbolic Easter story of them all.

Jesus showed himself again to the disciples by the Sea of Tiberius.
This time it was Jesus asking the questions.

Now here's a story.
Peter was a man consumed with shame and guilt.
He had disavowed his friendship with Jesus.
Worse yet,
he had done it at the time when Jesus was most in need of a friend.
It was a cowardly and inexcusable deed.
At the realization of what he had done,
    Peter went somewhere and wept like a child.
While he worked on his urban accent and his yuppie nonchalance,
    a rooster laughed.
    This hayseed Galilean heard it loud and clear.

He was an utterly dejected man.
But all of this was changed by one conversation with Jesus.
Peter found healing for his wounds and so can we. Love heals.
Jesus came "to break his fast" and dine with his friends, especially Peter.

He quietly asked Peter,
"Simon, son of John, do you love me more than these?" (John 21:15)

Do not dismiss this as a small thing. It was a miracle of sorts.
People disappoint and hurt one another and at times the wounds run deep.
They stand off and look at each other as strangers, or even enemies.
The only thing that can bridge the gap is forgiveness.
The two most difficult words to say are "I forgive,"
    and that is not easy when we have been deeply hurt.
If those two words are difficult for the offended party,
    they are no less difficult for the offender to hear.

You may sit there and think that it is glorious to be forgiven.
And in a sense, you are right.
But if you can say that flippantly,
    it inclines me to wonder if you have ever been forgiven.

It is not a light-hearted transaction
    to betray a friend,
    to feel ashamed,
    and then to be taken back and trusted once again.
That must surely be the most humbling experience a proud man can know.

Peter was a proud man.
Only a few days earlier, he had pledged his unfailing loyalty to Jesus.
In the presence of his fellow disciples he said,
"Lord, I am ready to go with you to prison and to death!" (Luke 22:33)
But when the chips were down,
Peter denied his friendship with Jesus.
He did it, not once, but three times.

Yet here he was being trusted and accepted by Jesus once again.

I am saying to you,
 that was not easy for Peter.
If there had been any other way out of his failure,
    I am certain he would have taken it.

But there was no other.
The only way out for Peter,
    or for anyone else,
        is contrition and forgiveness.

It will work for a husband and wife.
It will work for a parent and child.
It will work for any broken relationship.

Anytime, anywhere two people reconcile,
    healing takes place.
A great stone is rolled away.

The Risen Christ does not crush the fragile person.
He does not bruise the person who is afraid.
He does not abandon the person who has denied him.

Instead he lifts up the fallen through his healing love,
    and it is Easter all over again.

The cross is empty now.
There is no birth without an empty womb,
There is no Eucharist without an empty cross,
There is no Easter until our hearts are so empty
    that only the Spirit can fill them.
Then there are Alleluias everywhere.
Christ walks on all the Emmaus roads of our lives
    and calls us from the shore of every sea.
Easter empties all the tombs
    and fills the earth with angels of hope.

A Glimpse of Fr. Hayes

The man we honor today, Fr. Michael Hayes, reflects that spirit of intimacy with God more than any other priest I have known in forty-six years. While heads of corporations all over America are obsessed with control and mastery over people, and bishops, at least some of them, ride around in chauffeured cars, and priests lock themselves in rectories protected by secretaries and housekeepers, Mike Hayes is available in the local diner booth. I ask you honestly: if Jesus came back to the Duluth diocese, where would you find him—in the chancery office, in a chauffeured limo, or sitting vulnerable in a diner booth? You know the answer. That's why I say my friend and your pastor is a unique man of God. Where do you find his equal?

—Finbarr Corr, a seminary classmate,
on the occasion of Fr. Hayes' Jubilee Mass on June 11, 2000

Acts 13:14, 43–52; Rev 7:9, 14b–17; John 10:27–30

A Unique Voice

"My sheep hear my voice, I know them, and they follow me." (John 10:27)

The musical *Rent* was a highly successful
    and Pulitzer Prize-winning play of the 90s.
In fact, it was said to be the musical
    that saved Broadway from financial ruin.

The story was set in Manhattan's east side
    and told of life among people who were
    addicted, HIV positive, cross dressers,
    bisexual, and poor.
In some cities, *Rent* spawned a phenomenon
    known as Renter, Rent Heads, or Rent Rats.

These young people were fascinated by the play
    and would line up overnight in the cold
    to buy cheap last-minute tickets.
Some saw the show more than thirty times
    and knew the words of every lyric.
They would mimic the gestures and dance of every character
    and described themselves as living by the creed of the show.
 They clung to the theme as a guide for life,
"Forget regret. No day but today."
Some said the show was their church.

This story of Renters is a real-life story that is more than interesting.
It tells us of people who have heard something in the voices
    that have sung to them.
It tell us of people who have heard in those voices
    a message for their life.

The story of Renters probably stirs a host of reactions in us,
    especially sadness.

But it is an intriguing story to have in mind
    as we reflect on today's Scriptures about confusion and turmoil.

There is the one voice we need to hear,
    the voice of the true shepherd who calls his flock.

Renters was a group of young people searching for a truth.
But nowadays most of us find ourselves
    faced with competing sets of confusing ideas, values, and voices
        as we embark on the same search.

We live in an age of computers, e-mails, web pages,
    Ipods, and cell phones.
Thanks to cell phones, many people are never alone for long,
    never left with their own thoughts and ideas.

CDs, TVs, radios, magazines, junk mail, and opinion polls
    constantly bombard and manipulate us.

Print and talk show journalists, commentators, talk show hosts, and experts
    all constantly seek to persuade and influence us.
They are the "chattering class," as someone has called them.

Let's face it, our new information-based technology has brought us
    neither earthly bliss nor eternal salvation.
In a world with so much available information,
    it is difficult to know just what information
        should be central to our lives.
In a world with so many voices over so many cables and computers,
    we are beginning to wonder whose voice we should listen to.

The Church theological debates,
    once heard only in sacred halls,
    are now reported in *Time* and *Newsweek*.

The secret sins of the Church's shepherds
   are now featured on the nightly news.

There are many interesting voices in the Church as well.

There are the voices of the late Mother Teresa
   and of Mother Angelica,
   of Cardinal O'Connor and Fr. Andrew Greeley,
   of differing bishops and their pastors.
We hear our chief shepherd, our pope,
   along with the echo of John XXIII
   still resounding in many ears.

Our Father's house contains many shepherds and shepherdesses,
 and it is not easy listening to them all.
We need to reach for a central idea, a direction, a voice.
We need a voice that will hold it all together.

There were conflicting voices in Jesus' time as well.

Some said he was the Messiah, while others doubted this fact.
When the folks from Jerusalem asked him
   to state once and for all if he really was the Messiah,
   he fired back that they should know better than to ask.
After all, hadn't they seen for themselves
   the works he had done in his Father's name?

Then Jesus used language and imagery
   that needed no explanation in his time.
"My sheep hear my voice. I know them, and they follow me."
   (John 10:27)
The people knew how flocks of sheep mingled together in the hills
   until the moment each shepherd called out to his particular flock
   with a unique voice.

I am uncomfortable thinking of the Church in terms of sheep,
   because of what I know about them.

But I am convinced that in a world
    that places such a premium on information
    and in a Church with so many voices,
        we need to listen in a new way
            to the unique voice of our true Shepherd, Jesus.

Just as Jesus heard the voice of the Father,
    so the disciples of Jesus
        will hear the distinctive voice of the Good Shepherd.

Danish philosopher Soren Kierkegaard reminds us,
    "There is no lack of information in the Christian land;
        something else is lacking."

We can learn from the old metaphor that Jesus used
    and listen intently from time to time, amid all the voices,
    to the Shepherd who calls out to each one of us
        with a still familiar voice.

We are called to follow him, not some idea about him.
If we listen to him, he will give us life, eternal life.

Acts 14:21–27; Rev 21:1–5a; John 13:31–33a, 34–35

No More Sea?

Today we continue to reflect on heaven,
    which is part of the gift of Easter,
    and the promise of the resurrection that Jesus has given us.

In the second reading, from Revelation,
    a visionary poet gives us neither a definition nor ideas
        but an image of heaven
        as a city where God lives with his people.

Let's listen again to the reading.

"Then I saw a new heaven and a new earth;
    for the first heaven and the first earth had passed away,
    and the sea was no more.
And I saw the holy city, the new Jerusalem,
    coming down out of heaven from God,
    prepared as a bride adorned for her husband.
And I heard a loud voice from the throne saying,
    'See, the home of God is among mortals.
He will dwell with them;
    they will be his peoples
    and God himself will be with them;
He will wipe every tear from their eyes.
Death will be no more;
    mourning and crying and pain will be no more,
    for the first things have passed away.'
And the one who was seated on the throne said,
    'See, I am making all things new.'" (Rev 21:1–5a)

Heaven is depicted here as a new set of relationships.
It is a relationship between us and God.

"They will be his peoples, and God himself will be with them."
   (John 21:3)

It is a relationship among us human beings,
   where mourning and pain will be no more. (John 21:4)

It is within each of us individually as well.
   Jesus said, "The Kingdom of God is within you,"
   and also that he came that each of us might have life,
   and have it more abundantly.

Heaven is found in the whole universe:
   "The first things have passed away."
   "See I am making all things new."

Heaven is probably, in some sense, a continuation of the present.

Can we experience a joy with God in heaven
   if we know nothing of joy and celebration here on earth?
Can we be open to God in the hereafter,
   if we are closed to God here?
If we shut out our neighbors on earth,
   can we be open in heaven to God who created them?

From the Revelation of John there is one strange phrase, however:
   "and the sea was no more."
No more sea?

For all of us who find the ocean to be a place of wonder and soul-refreshing,
   this does not sound heavenly at all.
We are the ones who pay premium dollars
   to get an ocean front room at the resort,
   who send post cards to loved ones with phrases like,
"It is so beautiful here, We are having the time of our lives.
   Wish you were here."

How could heaven be a place without a beautiful ocean—
    as in Lahinch, County Clare, my birthplace?

Think of the setting for the writer of Revelation.
John was imprisoned on an island
    off the coast of Asia Minor, or modern Turkey.

It was just across the water from the mainland,
    the place of freedom, of civilization, of Christian community,
        of continued ministry.
It was so close that he could see it,
    and when the wind was just right,
    he was so close he could even hear it,
    just like prisoners on Alcatraz,
    separated from freedom by the shark-infested waters of San Francisco Bay.
Being on such an island was pure torture.

John loved his churches. He missed them. He longed to be united with them.
Only one thing stood in his way: the sea.
And so, for John, heaven was "no more sea."

Do not worry, sea lovers.
Even if literally there is no ocean in heaven,
    you will not even realize it is gone.
If you could send a post card back from heaven,
    I am sure you would still say,

"It is so beautiful here. We are having the time of our lives.
    Wish you were here!"

Acts 15:1–2, 22–29; Rev 21:10–14, 22–23; Jn 14:23–29

Here's the Secret

I tune in to radio talk shows once in a while.
I cannot take a steady diet of it;
    music refreshes me more.

But talk-radio has a lot of energy.
One of the amazing things about it is
    how absolutely certain everybody is that what they are saying is true.
In talk-radio,
    there is usually no exploring of options or possibilities.
Instead people say
    this is the way it is;
    this is what I believe;
    and my opinion is unshakable.
Yet in real life, off the radio, we meet so few people like that.

Many people have fears, worries, and anxieties.
What am I to do?
What is right?
Whom should I believe?

The Scriptures we have heard today
    are a cleansing breath of fresh spring air.
They make clear that there are certain paths
    for believers who have doubts.
We can live and act in spite of doubt and uncertainty.
In fact,
    our doubts can strengthen rather than weaken our faith.

In today's gospel, Jesus said,
"Peace I leave with you; my peace I give to you.

I do not give to you as the world gives.
Do not let your hearts be troubled,
    and do not let them be afraid." (John 14:27)

The most striking thing about that statement
    is the setting in which it was made.

Jesus was spending one last evening with his friends.
On the surface, everything seemed tranquil and calm.
But that was an illusion.
In a few hours Jesus would be arrested and put to death.

It would be a total shock to his disciples.
But none of it would catch Jesus by surprise,
    he faced it with absolute calm.

He contrasted "my peace" that he was giving,
    to the peace of the world.
"I do not give to you as the world gives." (John 14:27)
What was the difference?

Whatever peace the world has is dependent on peaceful conditions.
The peace that Jesus possessed was effective in the midst of turmoil.
He knew the secret of being inwardly calm in chaotic times.

Those who sail the sea in ships have an old adage.
They say;
"The worst of storms can't sink a ship
    unless it gets on the inside."

The life of Jesus demonstrates the truth of that saying,
    especially during his final week.
The storm was raging all around him,
    but it never penetrated his heart and mind.

He was surrounded by fear.
Pilate was afraid for his position.
The priests were afraid for their power.

The disciples were afraid for their lives.
Fear was everywhere.

But the fear never got inside of him.

He was surrounded by hate.
The Jewish priests hated the Romans.
The Romans hated the Jewish priests.
And that final week
    the Jewish priests and Romans joined forces in hating Jesus.

But the hate never got inside of him.

This is truly an incredible thing.
And what is even more incredible,
    Jesus offered this same composure to you and me.
    "My peace I give to you."

What is the secret, Jesus' secret, of being inwardly calm in chaotic times?
Part of it is caring about something greater than yourself.

If my primary concern is me,
    and your primary concern is you,
    we are going to spend a lot of time being upset.

Jesus cares about his friends more than he cares about himself.
It was this kind of commitment that enabled Jesus to remain calm.
When you and I care about someone else
    more than we care about ourselves, personal setbacks will not destroy us.
We can handle them for the sake of those we love.
The amazing composure of Jesus
    was his firm faith in the power of right.
That faith took the sense of desperation out of his life.

Jesus had a strong sense of responsibility,
    but he kept it within manageable limits.
He did not feel that everything depended on him.

The destiny of the world was not in his hands;
    it was in his Father's hands.
Jesus left it there and that gave him an inner calm,
    even in the chaos of Calvary.

The terrorist attacks of 9/11 affected not only the entire nation
    but the world.
Lives were lost, hearts were broken, and millions shared in our grief.
It was a horrible crime and an unspeakable tragedy.
It shook our illusion of a safe haven.
We had thought of terrorism as something
    that happened on the other side of the world.
9/11 gave us the feeling that everything was spinning out of control.
But that also is an illusion.

Remember Jesus on the last night of his life;
    his whole life seemed to be blowing apart.
But the storm never got inside of him because, above all else,
    he trusted God.
Ultimately, that is the secret of being inwardly calm
    in a chaotic world.

Hear and receive the gentle words of Jesus,
"Peace I will leave with you,
    my peace I will give to you." (John 14:27)

A Glimpse of Fr. Hayes

Fr. Hayes was close to all our children, but when our daughter, Jenny, and her unborn child, were killed in a violent car accident in Arizona, he was moved to tears. Her funeral homily was delivered just before the Winter Olympics in January of 2002 and it ended like this:

Jenny carries with her all that is life and holds the torch aloft lighting the way for others. No matter when her flame fell, it would have been too soon. Hers was a great spirit and it created a way of life. She possessed that indestructible spark.

Look around you, Jennie. Look at all the torches you have lit and all the lives you have touched, all the paths you have brightened. The Olympic flame will go out in six weeks, but your flame will burn brightly forever.

To finish, I would like to misquote Shakespeare's Hamlet *if I may.*

"Oh Jennie, farewell sweet princess,

May flights of angels sing thee to thy rest."

—Irene McKay, Parishioner of St. Francis and Holy Trinity, Barnum, MN

Acts 7:55–60; Rev 22:12–14, 16–17, 20; John 17:20–26

Where Have All the Stars Gone?

History says, Don't hope
On this side of the grave,
But then, once in a lifetime
The longed-for tidal wave
Of Justice can rise up,
And hope and history rhyme.

So hope for a great sea-change
On the far side of revenge.
Believe that a farther shore
is reachable from here.
Believe in miracles
And cures and healing
wells.
– Seamus Heaney, *The Cure at Troy*

Ever since Shakespeare's Mark Antony stood up to say
"Friends, Romans, Countrymen…"
eulogies have been the trickiest of all speeches.
Mark Antony began by saying that he had
"come to bury Caesar, not to praise him."
But by the end of his eulogy,
he had convinced the crowd that Caesar was not only a ruler
but a god.

You notice similar eulogies written by journalists
who mourn the passing of Hollywood stars.
The stars are canonized as the "world's greatest,"

always the superlative,
always the most,
always the best.

These modern-day Mark Antonys try to convince us
    that we will never gaze on such stars again.
"Where have all the stars gone, long time passing?"
There is something terribly depressing in this kind of talk.
What seems missing is hope for the future.

We sometimes hear that kind of "lost hope" talk from priests
who mourn the passing of the kind of Church
    they once knew and loved and served.

They realize that our seminaries and convents
    are becoming like those old dilapidated motels
    where the neon sign forever blinks: Vacancy.

When I was in the seminary in the late 1950s,
    there were over 50,000 seminarians.
The number today has dropped to less than 10,000.

Bishops, especially in larger dioceses, have closed once vibrant parishes
    because they simply do not have the priests to staff them.
There are storms of protest from people who picket the chancery offices.
People remember the good old days
    when their parish was the biggest and best in the diocese.
 How could the bishop be so cruel as to close
    St. Joseph's, St. Michaels's, St. Patrick's?

Cardinal Bernadin's predecessors had built the churches of Chicago
    but his job was to close them.
Building was easy; closing was like a death in the family.
Even after all his listening and deciding,
    his home was picketed after virtually every closing.

Some bishops have now appointed women as parish life coordinators
    instead of closing parishes.
Maybe these are the bishops
who notice the line in the Easter reading from the Acts of the Apostles,
    "There were some women in their company..."

But look for a great sea change when hope and history rhyme.
Believe that a farther shore is reachable from here.
Believe in miracles
    and cures and healing wells.

Not everyone is pessimistic about the Church's future.
Once in a while someone will stand up and dare to speak words
    that are both realistic and hopeful.
They are like the poets who end their eulogies by telling us,
    "The best is yet to be."

They leave us with a sense of hope in the future.
They don't tell us to just "hang in there,"
    but rather to believe in the wonder of God's spirit
    who makes all things new.

Whatever happened to
    "Behold! I am with you always even to the end of the world?"

What's most striking in the gospel that we read today
    is that the prayer of Jesus before his death
    expresses not just his trust in the Father,
    but also his trust in his disciples.

Jesus did not dwell on past glories.
He looked at those who prayed with him,
    a weak and motley little group.
But Jesus believed that those eleven really did belong to the Father,
    and that through those "earthen vessels" his work would carry on.
Jesus prayed for his disciples because he believed "the best was yet to be."

This prayer of Jesus from the Scriptures is like the Bible itself.
It is never a closed book of past events,
    but a book that is open towards the future.
It is a book about God's promises.

The God of the Bible never tells us all the stars have gone,
    but rather bids us to pray for those who have yet to shine.

Acts 2:1–11; 1 Cor 12:3b–7, 12–26; Jn 20:19–23

Ever Ancient, Ever New, Ever Beautiful

There is a quality of human life that is wild and irrepressible.
It invites us to dance
  when we are lame and arthritic.
It wants us to sing
  when our voices are choked and sobbing with grief.
It wants us to stare
  into the face of hopelessness and smile.
It plants a flower in the wilderness.

We find in the solemnity of Pentecost,
  the God Spirit who defies description.
Writers fall back on words like
  fire, wind, breath, and each one of these hint at ferment
    and unpredictability.

Still, when we think of the Spirit of God as fire or wind,
  we would prefer it to be contained.
Comfortable armchair Christians
  would be happy with the Spirit as fire
    if it were the gentle log fire in a winter fireplace.

The Spirit as wind would be acceptable
  if it were the balmy breeze on a summer beach,
  gently filling the sails of the boats on the lake.

"Come, Holy Spirit"
  is a dangerous prayer if we are not prepared for the consequences.
We would have to get ready for the rush of God
  which could tear through our tidy lives and their sheltered places.

Paul, who was familiar with the prompting of the Spirit,
    tells us simply that "God's gift was not a Spirit of timidity,
        but the Spirit of power and love and self-control."

The Spirit may become an uncomfortable and embarrassing companion,
    for we could be led to reckless generosity in the face of hunger.

We may be propelled towards forgiveness
    when revenge would be a sweeter solution.

We may be moved with compassion at the sight of the homeless
    when it would be easier to walk right on by.

The Spirit may drag
    the well-ordered, respectable, church-going Christian into action!

It has been over 2000 years since the first Pentecost,
    and the Church is still being born in each one of us.
"She is ever ancient, ever new, ever beautiful,"
    according to Augustine.

Despite our weaknesses, our sin, and our fears,
the Church continues to survive and grow
    as it reaches out to the ends of the earth.

On this Pentecost Sunday each of us is invited to open ourselves to the
    power of the Spirit in our lives.

We are more than a collection of individuals; we are the Church.
Let us spell the words of Church very carefully together.
C H U R C H.
"U R" is at the center of the Church!
We are brought together to be of service to one another.

How could we hold this good news to ourselves?
Jesus breathed the Spirit upon the disciples,
    but he did not mean for them to hold their new breath.

Breath in…receive the Holy Spirit.
Breathe out…give that gift away to the world.
Do not use your breath to blow out the fire
   but instead use it to fan the flames.

Even as we mark with solemnity this feast of Pentecost,
lines from Shakespeare's *Tempest* come to mind.

"Our revels now are ended. These our actors,
As I foretold you, were all spirits, and
Are melted into air, into thin air:
And, like the baseless fabric of this vision,
The cloud-capped towers, the gorgeous palaces,
The solemn temples, the great globe itself,
Yea, all which it inherit, shall dissolve,
And, like this insubstantial pageant faded,
Leave not a rack behind."
—Act IV Sc1

Our Easter revels are now ended on this Pentecost,
   the last day of the high season of our faith.
We will retire the Easter Candle to the baptistery
   where it will light the baptisms we celebrate
      throughout the coming year.
Easter flowers and Easter songs
   will share the fate of Shakespeare's "cloud-capped towers"
   and "solemn temples" dissolved, not leaving a rack behind.

As we descend this day from Easter's lofty plateau
   into the valley of "Ordinary Time" and everyday life,
we carry with us the vision that has sustained us these past fifty days.

The melody lingers,
the scent clings,
the emotions remain.
We cannot help but remain an Easter people.

As true of many farewell traditions, we receive today a going-away present.
The God who has blessed us gives us a final blessing, the gift of the Spirit.

Who is the Spirit?

Several years ago a missionary in China
built a small church for his new Christians.
On an inside wall of the church, he drew a huge triangle
    to stand for the Holy Trinity.
In the first corner of the triangle,
    he drew an eye, symbolizing God the Father.
In the second corner of the triangle,
    he drew a cross, symbolizing God the Son.
In the third corner of the triangle,
    he drew a dove, symbolizing God the Holy Spirit.

After he had finished the drawing,
    an old Chinese woman came up to him and said:
"Honorable Father and his eye I understand.
    Honorable Father sees everything we do.
Honorable Son and his cross I understand.
    Honorable Son died on the cross for us.
But honorable Holy Spirit and his bird I do not understand."

    Little boy: The Holy Spirit is a bird.
    Teacher: Why do you say that?
    Little boy: You call it the parakeet! (paraclete)

One of the Bible's best depictions of the Spirit comes in John's gospel.
Speaking to Nicodemus, Jesus likens the Spirit to wind.

"The wind blows where it chooses and you hear the sound of it,
    but you do not know where it comes from, or where it goes.
So it is with everyone who is born of the Spirit." (John 3:8)

Scripture also connects love with the Spirit in St. Paul's writings,
"God's love has been poured into our hearts
    through the Holy Spirit that has been given to us." (Rom 5:5)

The Christian prayer says,
"Come, Holy Spirit, fill the hearts of your faithful,
    and kindle in them the fire of your love."

Whenever human beings come together in love,
    the Holy Spirit is present and active in and through their love:
    the love of man and woman,
    parent and child,
    friend and friend,
    priest and people.
Whenever creative love enriches life, the Spirit is present and operating.

The Christian prayer goes on:
"Send forth your Spirit and they shall be created,
    and you shall renew the face of the earth.

That prayer refers to more than the world of nature.

Our social world also needs renewal.
Some of our economic, cultural, and political social systems
    are ravaged by our sinfulness, greed, and injustice.
We encounter the Holy Spirit in all those who resist these evils
    and do the work of justice and peace.

Opportunities for encountering the Spirit are as broad as the world itself.
We cannot confine the Spirit to sacred moments or sacred places.

To be sure, the Spirit is present in our prayer and worship.
But the Creator Spirit pervades all of life
    and may be encountered in all of creation:
    natural, personal, and social.

Dare we go forth from this Pentecost with enough faith
to seize the opportunities the Spirit offers us?

Prov 8:22–31; Rom 5:1–5; Jn 16:12–15

The Trademark of Our Faith

Most of the feasts of the Church year center on events
    like Christmas and Easter.
But today and next Sunday we celebrate "idea feasts"
    highlighting particular truths of faith.

Today we gather to give thanks and praise for the Triune God.
This feast is well-placed, coming immediately after Pentecost.
We have now completed the celebration of our salvation story realized
    by God the Father,
        through the Son,
            in the Holy Spirit.
Our God is three-in-one.

I like what Gregory of Nyssa has to say about efforts to describe the Trinity.

First, they reminded him of the inarticulate mumbo-jumbo of a mother
    trying to communicate to her baby in an imagined way.

Second, he likened them to hog-calling language.

Third, they reminded him of someone rolling-home drunk,
    whose wobbly language and slurred speech
        barely seem to communicate at all.

Does this mean we go back to the triangle or shamrock and admit defeat?
We are warned against summing up the mystery accurately.

Perhaps what matters more
    is that babies realize that they are loved
        and that hogs and drunks get home safely.

So we just struggle to find helpful words and images
    to express our faith in the Trinity.

It is good that we have this annual solemnity in honor of the Holy Trinity.
It causes us to reflect on God's inner life.

We don't bother too much to reflect about what God is like.
What God is like is not so much a matter for understanding
    as it is for imagination.
However, since faith is a matter of truth,
    we usually don't associate imagination with it.
But imagination is the power to create the images we need
    to understand life
        and to make sense of our experiences.

Imagination gives us a picture
    of what God is asking of us in the big picture.

What if we imagine a God who cares about us
    more than we care for ourselves,
    more than we care for those we love?

Lack of imagination is part of our problem these days
    in both the Church and society.

Liberals and conservatives fight
    not about God, but about images of God,
    not about truth, but about explanations of truth.

Conservatives whine, "We've always done it this way."
Liberals cry, "Let the new times roll."
Traditionalists cower in fear, that if we change one jot or tittle,
    God will punish us.
Progressives naively think that if we build a bigger ball field,
    shoeless Jesus Christ will come and play with us.

But imagination is not fantasy.
It is the power to create images
    that explain life
        and paint pictures of God.

Some people blame science for deadening our imagination
    and that may be true up to a point.
When we calculate and count everything,
    we forget that truth is more than facts.
Reality is larger than data,
    but serious science now knows that.

I have a favorite scientific mystery and it has to do with electrons.
Paired electrons move in opposite directions,
    and if you change the direction of one,
        the other changes direction, too.

Now send one electron north at the speed of light
    and the other south at the speed of light.
They are now traveling away from each other at twice the speed of light
    with no possible means of contact.

Then change the direction of one and the other one will change direction.
Imagine the incredible power
    that makes these two absolutely independent units
        move in tandem like that.
The universe is a product of imagination, God's imagination.

In the scientific world, we have only seen a little of what God can do
    because our scientific knowledge is limited.

Our faith gives us a tantalizing glimpse into God's inner life,
    a relational life,
        and how much God is revealed as God-for-us.
These morsels should tempt us
    to explore the mystery further
        with our imaginations.

We can nibble at its meaning.
We can place our emotional arms around it,
    but we will never be able to sink our teeth
        entirely into the depth and breadth of it.

On Trinity Sunday we encounter God
    with a sense of awe, wonder, and mystery.
However, we are challenged to approach our God that way
    not just on this Sunday but every day of the year.

It is this great mystery
    that we celebrate,
    that we profess each time we sign ourselves with the cross.

In fact it has become the trademark of our faith.
In the name of the Father and of the Son and of the Holy Spirit. Amen.

Ex 24:3–8; Heb 9:11–15; Mk 14:12–16, 22–26

We Are What We Have Received

On this special solemnity called the Body and Blood of Christ,
    we shall do what the Lord commanded:
    "Take and eat…take and drink."
Listen to what the Christians of the fourth century did
    as described by the Bishop of Jerusalem:

"When you come up to receive…
    make your left hand a throne for the right
    (for it is about to receive a King),
    cup your palm,
    and so receive the body of Christ;
    then answer 'Amen.'
Carefully hallow your eyes by the touch of the sacred body,
    and then partake, taking care to lose not one part of it.
Such a loss would be like a mutilation of your own body.
Why, if you had been given gold dust, would you not take the utmost care
    to hold it fast, not letting a grain slip through your fingers,
    lest you be so much the poorer?
How much more carefully, then,
    you guard against losing so much as a crumb of that
    which is more precious than gold or precious stones!

After partaking of the body of Christ,
    also the chalice of his blood,
    bow in a posture of worship and reverence as you say, "Amen,"
    and sanctify yourself by receiving also the blood of Christ.

While it is still warm upon your lips,
    moisten your fingers with it
    and so sanctify your eyes,
    your forehead, and the other organs of sense.
Then wait for the prayer and give thanks to the God
    who has deigned to admit you to such high mysteries…"

Today, in this church,
    the first century, the fourth century, and the twenty-first century
        come together.

The details differ from the upper room,
    coursing through the Church of Jerusalem, to us,
    but the reality is the same.

This solemnity of the Body and Blood of Christ
    invites us to consider
        the truly outstanding actions that we perform here.
These actions transform us and our world.

Our presence here is a privilege, not just a duty.

The reality is expressed, simply and profoundly by Jesus himself:
    "This is my body…, This is my blood."
We call it the Real Presence.

In the Eucharist, Jesus is present and his presence is real;
    not that his presence in our hearts,
    in the gathered assembly,
    and in the proclaimed Word is not real.

This presence is something special, unique
 for it speaks of a distinct relationship with Jesus' flesh and blood.
"My flesh is food indeed and my blood is drink indeed."
And Jesus says, "Unless you eat my flesh and drink my blood
    you have no life in you."

It does not mean your heart will stop beating,
   or your brain will cease to function if you do not eat it.
It means that the life of Jesus will not course through you
   the way he intended it should.

Here is a food, which has the potential for giving life
   that is unparalleled.

Augustine wrote:
"I am the food of grown men and women;
   grow and you shall eat me
   and you shall not change me into yourself the way bodily food acts:
You shall be changed into me."

In the words of Pope Pius XII:
"If you have received worthily,
   you are what you have received.
You are Christ.
You can expect to live the life of the earth-bound Jesus."

It is one thing to compliment ourselves on being Christ
   but are we?
Are we really what we have received?

In Catholicism, the Bread of Life is not primarily an indivdualistic thing,
   a solitary supper, my private party,
   something between "Jesus and me."
Its function is to form community.

Paul phrased it beautifully:
"Because the bread is one, we, though many, are one body,
   for we all partake of the one bread."

The Lord who locks himself in the tabernacle of my body
   is none other than the Lord
   who nourishes my nextdoor neighbor and a faraway pope.
The same Christ feeds people everywhere.

Christ is not divided and is not multiplied.
He is one and the same body; one and the same Christ.

In his flesh we are one,
    but are we?
When something divides us, we need to ask the question:
    Was it for this that the Word-Made-Flesh
    offered his flesh and blood
    when he said, "This is my body which is given for you"?

There is a world beyond our altars.
The Christ of Holy Thursday not only feeds us,
    he also does with us today what he did that night with the bread.
He takes us.
He blesses us.
He breaks us,
    and he gives us to others.

We are what we have received.
We are Christ.
This should expand our horizons.

This reality forces us to focus on the hungers of the human family.
Millions of men, women, and children
    struggle desperately to live dignified lives, struggle even to live.
Just talking about the Bread of Life
    can sound awfully empty and suspiciously hollow.
Our words will be empty and
    pointless,
    unless we who feed on the Eucharistic Christ
        become Eucharist for the life of the world.
Our feeding on the flesh and blood of Christ
    must take us from this Church into the world.

We must be really present in the world,
    not merely our money or our minds,
    because as Christians, as Christ,
    our lives are love and only love can bring life.

Only love can light dulled eyes with hope
  or can promise somebody, somewhere,
    that tomorrow will be more human and more worth living.

"You need to dismiss the people," the disciples tell Jesus.
"There is no place to stay, nothing to eat around here.
 Send them to the towns and farms nearby
    that they may find food and lodging."

But Jesus replied, "You give them something to eat."

A Glimpse of Fr. Hayes

During our last visit with Fr. Mike, my wife and I were entertained with jokes, advice, stories, and more. One of the stories Fr. Mike told was about a Tinker's funeral he had in Ireland.

By definition, Tinker is a shortening of the Gaelic word "Tinceard," which means tinsmith. It was commonly used to describe an Irish Traveler or Gypsy, although many now consider it an insult.

Apparently, when a Tinker dies, other Tinkers mourn the loss by a celebration that typically includes consumption of large volumes of alcohol. The funeral was on a Sunday, so by Friday the Tinkers began arriving in town to start their mourning libations. By the time of the funeral, so much celebrating had been done that Fr. Mike was giving the sermon to those sleeping on the ground and resting against the headstones. My impression was that Fr. Mike thoroughly enjoyed the experience.

—Chris and Katie Pfahl, former St. Francis parishioners, Carlton, MN

Ordinary Time

Isa 62:1–5; 1 Cor 12:4–11; Jn 2:1–11

The New Wine of Grace

January is an ice-box month in Minnesota.
Gray skies and bitter winds dampen our spirits.
Our mailboxes no longer bulge with cheery Christmas cards.
January's mail can provide the dreaded Visa bill and our 1040 forms.
And there are no more Viking games.

This morning John the Evangelist
    tells us a story to thaw our January hearts
        and give us hope.

We know that more than any other of the evangelists,
    John was a poet.
And so his story of Cana is filled with poetic meaning.

Miracles for John were not just miracles,
    but signs of something deeper.

Today's changing of the water into wine was the first sign
    that God's power is truly at work in Jesus.
We don't know who the couple was,
    maybe because this wasn't just their wedding,
    but also the new marriage between God
        and the people of God.

Another poet, Isaiah had dreamed about this day when he said,

"As the bridegroom rejoices
    over the bride,
So shall your God rejoice
    over you." (Isa 62:5)

For John, Jesus is not just a guest at the wedding;
    he is the bridegroom who has come to make
        a loving and lasting
            commitment with God's people.

Even the fact that there were six water jars
    had a deeper meaning for John.
For Jews, seven was the complete and perfect number
    while the number six signified something incomplete.

The six water jars meant
    that Israel's days were running short,
    that a new age was at hand,
    when Jesus would do away with the
        imperfections and restrictions of the law
    and bring the new wine of grace that was available to all.

And so we see that the more we delve
    into the deeper meanings of the story of Cana,
    the more we learn who Jesus is,
    and what God invites us to do.

Pope John XXIII shocked the Church
    when he announced that he would convoke an ecumenical council,
    Vatican II in 1963.
He felt trapped by the Curia.
He once told Cardinal Cushing of Boston,
    "I'm in a bag here."

The Curia cardinals were shocked
    and protested that they could not possibly be prepared
    to have a council by 1963.
"All right, then," John responded, "We'll have it in 1962."

The stories of Cana and of Vatican II are all about newness,
    new wine, new grace,
    and new beginnings.

The story of Cana is like the story of John XXIII
    because new life comes at a time
    when spirits are drooping,
    when folks are embarrassed,
    old, alone, trapped,
       when the wine has run out.

Listen to the voices of people who are trapped.

    "Ah, why should I vote? It doesn't matter who wins."
    "After all these years, I'm not going to change."
An old man sighs,
    "It doesn't matter any more; my life is almost over.
A young girl complains,
    "The same old thing; this place is boring."
The cleric laments,
    "Rome isn't going to change. I might as well give up."
The husband or wife admits,
    "I guess we're just stuck in a rut."

Tomorrow we celebrate the birthday of Martin Luther King, Jr.
    Dr. King never moaned about the fact
    that the wine of freedom was drying up in America.
He deeply believed in the power of God's grace,
    not only to change water into wine,
    but to change hearts of stone
    into hearts of flesh.

Here is a story about a young woman, Mary McAleese,
    who became President of Ireland in November of 1997.

Mary experienced prejudice from the South of Ireland
    because she was from the North, born in Belfast,
    even though she had lived for twenty years in Dublin.
In the North her family experienced appalling persecution
    because they were Catholic.

Two of her best friends were murdered on her wedding day,
    her father's pub was blown up,
        her deaf brother was beaten to death,
        and her family was eventually intimidated
        to the extent that they had to leave their house.

And here she was on Inauguration Day, November 11, 1997.
Mary McAleese was like new wine
    "with beaded bubbles winking at the brim," she told the nation.

"Ireland sits tantalizingly ready to
    embrace a golden age of affluence,
    self assurance, tolerance, and peace.
May I ask those of faith, whatever their faith may be,
    to pray for me and for our country."

It's been estimated that the new wine of Cana
    added up to one hundred and eighty gallons.
Once again the poet John was pointing to a deeper reality:
    the grace of Christ is inexhaustible.

There is still time for all of us
    as individuals,
    as a church,
    as a nation,
        to change and believe in the new wine
            that Jesus still pours out for us.

We follow a Lord who changes things:
    water into wine,
    bread into his body,
    old ways into new life,
        and January into hope.

"Joy is the infallible sign of the presence of God."
—Georges Bernanos

Neh 8:2–4a, 5–6, 8–10; 1 Cor 12:12–30; Luke 1:1–4, 4:14–21

Will the Real Jesus Please Stand Up?

If Jesus were born in our time,
    many of us by now would have snapshots and videos of him
    as he made his way around the countryside.
As it is, we have no pictorial representations at all
    from any point in Jesus' life.
But that has not stopped artists down through the ages
    from attempting to picture him.

The first Christians, however,
    were not so much interested in how Jesus looked
    as in what he did.

We may want to know:
    was he tall or short?
    dark-haired or light?
    how did he walk and move?
    was his voice deep?

The four gospels will not answer these questions for us,
    but they do give us a profile of Jesus.

There are four distinct approaches to Jesus in the four gospels.
These are different,
    but they do give us a handle
    on how Jesus impressed those who knew him.

The earliest picture is from the gospel of Mark.

This Jesus is
    a lean, gaunt figure;
    A hurried man always just one step ahead of his persecutors.
    His expression appears sad.
    His walk is rapid.
    He is a lonely man
        and a loner.

He is not very good company,
but when you are in pain,
you will easily recognize him.
In the gospel of Mark, he is a man of sorrows.

In the gospel of Matthew, Jesus appears
    more relaxed, calmer,
        a little aloof,
        rather professional.
    He is, in fact, a teacher.
    He takes pleasure in instructing people.

And like any good teacher, he is
    sometimes patient,
        sometimes demanding,
        sometimes agreeable,
    and sometimes argumentative.

When you are in the mood
    to learn a thing or two about life or death,
    Jesus is your man in the gospel of Matthew.

Jesus according to the gospel of Luke
    is a nice fellow.
He goes to weddings (Cana).
He drinks a little
    and cries a little.
He has rich friends.
He has poor friends.

He has the leisure to notice lilies and sparrows,
  and he can tell a good story
  about runaway boys and lost sheep.
He has something of the poet about him.
  He likes women and children.
So if you long to have a good, all-around human being for company,
  Jesus makes a fine friend in the gospel of Luke.

The gospel of John gives us yet another profile.
Here Jesus loses his humanity and takes on the glow of divinity.
  Nothing bothers this Jesus,
  and no one crosses him either.
  He is in complete charge at all times.
  He even decides when he will allow people to kill him.
  His death is not a defeat, but an hour of triumph.
  In this gospel, Jesus fairly sparkles with majesty.
So if you are not sure about God, this Jesus will straighten you out!

Will the real Jesus please stand up?

The reason for these four portraits
  is that one would not do Jesus justice.
And the reason there are no more than these four
  is because no number of pictures could encompass all of him.
Therefore we are free to choose
  the picture we like.
That is important because each of us needs a different Jesus.
Because he came to save us from the things we need to be saved from,
  each of us has his or her own different set of problems and needs—
  to which Jesus is the solution.
Each of us also needs a different Jesus at different times in our lives.

Sometimes
  we need someone to give us a little advice as in Matthew,
  we need someone to suffer with us as in Mark,
  we need someone to remind us of God, and we turn to John,
  or sometimes we just need a friend, and Luke's Jesus will be there.

Jesus is the one, as he himself said in today's gospel,
    "to bring good news to the poor,
    to let the oppressed go free,
    to proclaim the year of the Lord's favor." (Luke 4:18)

He is Good News,
    freedom and favor from God.
That really is enough of a portrait
    because it allows us to recognize Jesus anywhere.

I mentioned VCRs and photos earlier.
Well, going to a friend's house and viewing home videos
    for many people is regarded as one of the world's dullest evenings.
One thing can change our feelings,
    however, and that is if some of the shots happen to include us.
When you find yourself in a picture,
    it ceases to be a dull evening and becomes an interesting experience.

So it is with reading or listening to the Scriptures.
A movie becomes interesting when you identify with the characters involved
    and put yourself into the story.
A novel becomes interesting when you live the plot in your own mind.
The Bible can and should be taken just as personally.
It is a book about people and their experiences with God.
Look closely and you may start to recognize some of the people.
There is, in fact, a good chance you may find your own name
    on nearly every page.

Jer 1:4–5, 17–19; 1 Cor 12:31—13:13; Luke 4:21–30

Homeward Bound

Today Jesus goes home.
He goes back to Nazareth and re-enters the currents
that nurtured what he has become.

He strolls down the village streets to the synagogue,
    which literally means a gathering place,
    and takes in hand the scroll of the Sacred Scriptures.
He unrolls it to the holy Words of the prophet Isaiah's poetry and reads,
    "The Spirit of the Lord is upon me." (Luke 4:18)

And Jesus really means "me," himself.

The carpenter's son comes home to hold up a text from Scripture to say,
    "I am the one described here.
    I am that person chosen.
    Is anyone here overjoyed?"

In the ancient Mediterranean world,
    everyone had a proper place that was established by birth.
No one was ever expected to become something better than,
    or to improve on the lot of, their parents.
This is the basic foundation of honor:
    each child inherits, carries on, and is expected
    to safeguard the family's honor.

The people of Nazareth, Jesus' hometown,
    knew Jesus and his family very well.
"All spoke well of him and were amazed at the gracious words that came from
his mouth. They said, 'Is not this Joseph's son?'" (Luke 4:22)

Jesus stirred controversy, at the very least,
    because he did not seem to be carrying on Joseph's trade.
He did something different, which was a breach of family honor.

Instead of practicing his father's trade,
    Jesus preached in the synagogue.
    But more importantly, they knew
     that he practiced healing activities in the neighboring villages.
Yet in the Mediterranean world,
    the basic rule was "Look after your family first."

Jesus had broken this rule.
He healed the sick of Capernaum,
    but apparently had not healed anyone in his hometown.
He ministered, not just to Mediterranean Judeans
    but also to Gentiles, non-Jews, people not of his own kind.
To direct his healing activities to such as these
    was to transgress family honor very seriously.

Rubbing salt into the wound opened by his insulting behavior,
    he boldly claimed that he was doing just as Elijah and Elisha had done.

"When people heard this, all in the synagogue were filled with rage."
(Luke 4:28)
The shocking behavior of the adult Jesus is difficult for us to appreciate.
In our culture, children are expected to do better than their parents,
    go out on their own and live independent lives.

In TV ads the elderly insist,
    "I do not want to be a burden to my children."

How very different from the culture of the family and townsfolk of Jesus!

Jesus got the reception we would have expected
    from people whose horizons never extended
        beyond the view from the hill on which their town was built.

In fact, they jostled Jesus to the very edge of that hill
    and if it were not for his mysterious escape,
    Jesus would have ended his public career early on the hill of Nazareth,
    rather than later on the hill of Calvary.

I like to think he escaped because of the sheer force of his personality.
He turned; they backed away. Nobody dared to touch him.

There is a bleak irony and sad sarcasm here.
Jesus learned he no longer had a home.

Later, he would envy foxes in their "dens,"
    and acknowledge that he really had nowhere to call "home"
    where he could lay his head.

Today, Jesus comes home
    and he finds that he has moved,
    but they have not.

Jesus claimed to be under the influence of God's Spirit
    and would act accordingly.
He would do this in plain sight
    with things
        as real as sin,
        and hurting bodies,
        and anxious minds,
        and unrolled scrolls,
        and upturned tables,
        and wood,
        and bread and wine,
    and, of course, death and resurrection.

So here's the question!
Does Jesus have a home here in our midst, in our families, in our church?

He has been looking for a real home ever since that day in Nazareth.

You see, today's gospel, as in every gospel reading, is about us.
It was Jesus who unrolled the scroll here today and boldly announced,
"Today this Scripture has been fulfilled in your hearing." (Luke 4:21)

How do we react?
Do we welcome him home
    to our Table today?
Would anything, anyone,
    have to change for him to be comfortable here?
Is your home his?

Isa 6:1–2a, 3–8; 1 Cor 15:1–11; Luke 5:1–11

Send Me

There is a scale of belief and unbelief,
    and people are found at every level on that scale.
Besides the extreme doubters,
    there is a solid core of sane believers,
    as well as a large group we might label the credulous.
These people simply have to believe.

They itch to hear about the latest
    rumor of angels, miraculous healings,
        apparitions of Mary, or the newest near-death experiences.

In the early 1990s, an American living in Rome
    read about a woman from the Adriatic city of Pescara
    who claimed she had seen the Blessed Virgin Mary.
This woman announced that on a certain Sunday between noon and sunset,
    the Fatima miracle of the whirling sun would repeat itself at Pescara.

A Jesuit priest (of all people) believed her story
    and aided in spreading the news of the immanent miracle.
On that Sunday about 10,000 people from all over Europe arrived,
    awaiting the miracle on the hill of Pescara.
The American in Rome did not really believe that anything would happen,
    but made sure she was at St. Peter's Square at noon, just in case!

Nothing happened
    and the next day the matter was an object of bitter ridicule
        in the secular press.
But such disappointments don't even make a dent
    in those who love to believe.

They sit back, make excuses,
    and wait for the next time.

One non-believer said,
    "Catholics love Mary so much that they see her everywhere.
        Perhaps it is that love that is the real miracle."

Where do you fit on the scale of belief and unbelief?
Are you an extreme doubter?
A solid-core sane believer? One who has to believe?

The following questions may help reveal where you stand,
    and these questions are all on the scale of belief.
What is your belief about the continuity of life?
Is it necessary to affirm an intelligent creator of the universe?
Does human life have a meaning?
Do you believe that the prayers of petition change anything?

Today, many people are at least tempted
    to answer all such questions in the negative.
Or, if answered in the affirmative, a doubt lingers.

This all leads to the liturgy of today.
The liturgy provides us with a decidedly different response of faith
    to human existence and its meaning.
In each reading we are brought into contact with people
    who have become aware of a call by God
    and as a result of this, radically changed their lives.

In the first reading, Isaiah hears the Lord call after he is purified.
The Lord asks,
    "Whom shall I send, and who will go for us?"
    And I (Isaiah) said, "Here am I; send me!" (Isaiah 6:8)

Paul reminds the Corinthians in the second reading
    of his own conversion in Damascus after he had persecuted the church,
        and he calls himself, "the least of the apostles." (1 Cor 15:9)

Paul speaks movingly of the saving power
   of the death and resurrection of the Lord.

In the gospel, through the great catch of fish,
   Peter, James and John gain insight into their own lack of belief
   and how the Lord desires to make up for their lack of belief
      by transforming them into fishers of humanity.

Each of these—Isaiah, Paul, Peter,
James and John—are called
   to give a simple expression to their faith.
They are to banish all doubt
   and leave everything to pursue that inner calling, their vocation.

It is clear that it is God who calls,
   and we are free to accept or refuse the invitation.
It is clear that once a person answers,
   God takes over in a wonderful fashion,
      and accomplishes wondrous deeds.

In reflecting upon today's readings,
   we must not fall into an error often repeated in the Church—
   of interpreting vocation in a narrow sense
   as applied exclusively to priests, sisters, and brothers.

On the contrary, by the Church putting these three readings together,
   we are reminded that we are all called.
Whether we are working in the world of business,
   or caring for a family at home, or doing what we do,
   we must all, in some degree and in different ways
      leave everything in order to follow Christ.

Even during Jesus' lifetime, people chose different ways to follow him.
Peter and Andrew left everything behind, home and family,
   in order to follow him.
Mary, Martha, and Lazarus remained at home.

Now it is not clear at all
    that Peter and Andrew were holier than the siblings of Bethany.
There is no evidence in the gospels that Mary, Martha, or Lazarus
    denied Jesus as Peter did.

Their discipleship was barely visible
    while that of Peter, James, and John was active and public,
        especially after the resurrection.

All were disciples.
They had experienced the call of Jesus and radically changed their lives.

That is the way we know they were Christians.
That is the way we will know we are Christians.

The image of fishing in today's gospel is a very apt way
    of expressing the lived reality of Christian life.

When we fish, we throw a line into the deep
    but don't know what is going on down there.
We wait above for a sign of something good happening:
    a wiggle or two, the darting of the float, a pull on the line.

The same is true in our personal spiritual life.
We are filled with hope, yet we often must wait, not knowing clearly
    what the Lord has in store for us.
Sometimes we wait a long time, years perhaps,
    wondering whether the Lord is there at all.
Then something occurs that reveals his presence.

Suddenly, there is a great catch of fish,
    perhaps more than we hoped for and in ways we hardly expected.

The God who appeared absent suddenly manifests himself.
And the words of the Lord to Isaiah resounds in our hearts,
    "Whom shall I send?" (Isaiah 6:8)
        and the answer will be, "Here am I; send me."

Jer 17:5–8; 1 Cor 15:1–11, 16–20; Luke 6:17, 20–26

Not the Income, but the Attitude

"Blessed are you who are poor…" (Luke 6:20)

In the novel *The Street Lawyer* by John Grisham,
    Michael accuses Warner, an Atlanta lawyer,
    of knowing nothing about poverty.
"Maybe I do." Warner says,
"For people like us, poverty is a cheap apartment,
    a used car with dents and dings, bad clothing,
    no money to travel and see the world,
    no money to save, or invest, no retirement, no safety net, nothing."
"Perfect," Michael says, "You just proved my point.
    You don't know a damned thing about poverty."

Jesus spoke often and with great passion
    about the real problems of this life.
It troubled him that some people had too little,
    while others had too much.
And he wondered why the rich were so reluctant to help the poor.
We can interpret this in such a way that it has nothing to do with us.
But let us try to hear what Jesus has to say about the rich and the poor.

Surely, Jesus could not have been talking about us.
He must have had in mind the most serious abusers of wealth.
We know who they are.

Take Saddam Hussein, for example, the former dictator of Iraq.
He had maybe a dozen luxurious presidential palaces
    scattered all over the country.

He could sleep in a different mansion every night for a week or two.
But many of his people lived in squalor.

Jesus was obviously talking about Saddam Hussein.

The only problem with this line of reasoning
    is that Saddam Hussein was not there.
As far as we know, not one filthy rich person was present
    when Jesus spoke that day.
His audience was made up of ordinary people like you and me.
And we consider ourselves anything but rich!
    Most of us believe we are in the middle class.

We have all of the things we need, and maybe a few of the luxuries.
But rich?
No, that word does not apply to us.

However, if Jesus spoke the words of today's gospel to ordinary people,
    they may apply to us.
It could be that we are the very people he had in mind.

Rich to him did not mean billionaires, or even millionaires.
Jesus did not know anyone with that much money.
To him, rich was anybody who could meet all of their needs,
    with a little left over.
His "woe" applied to those who could help someone else a little
    but did not.

"Blessed are you who are poor." (Luke 6:10)
Caution!

Poverty is not the passport to God's kingdom,
    yet much Christian spirituality has taught that it is.
In the past, at least, there was a lot of preaching
    that told us that the poor were especially blessed,
    that they were close to the cross of Christ,
    and that they should be thankful for that special privilege.

Dorothy Day would walk out at this point!

The kind of religion that assumes that the poor are blessed
    is to say that there is something holy about poverty.
The poor, in their suffering, are indeed close to the cross of Christ.
So who would change that?

But when we accept this kind of teaching,
    there are some things we aren't noticing.
Jesus died on the cross, but he didn't stay there.
He rose from the dead to share his new life
    with his friends through the ages.

If he ate with sinners, and touched lepers
    and was a friend with the poor and oppressed people,
    it was in order to change them and their situation.

When he said, "Blessed are you who are poor,"
    he didn't leave it at that.
He added "for yours is the kingdom of God." (Luke 6:20)

When he said, "Blessed are you who are hungry now,"
    he added, "for you will be filled." (Luke 6:21)

When he said, "Blessed are you who weep now,"
    he added, "for you will laugh." (Luke 6:22)

The blessedness of the poor, the hungry, the sorrowing,
    does not come from their poverty or hunger.
These things are wrong, yes,
    but real poverty comes from injustice,
        disaster, disease, and much more.

Their blessedness is not in the cross itself,
    which is an unspeakable instrument of torture.
But their blessedness comes in the love and courage,
    which took that dreadful way to newness of life for all people.

People who have a little security
    sometimes behave as if poverty were infectious.
If you touch the poor you'll catch it;
    and the poor, who are shunned like lepers,
    are blamed for their condition.

Those who have escaped the humiliating miseries of real poverty,
    and those who are not poor but always afraid of poverty,
    can easily slip into Luke's category of the rich.

It isn't the income;
    it's the attitude that incurs the danger of "woe."

Dorothy Day once said,
    "Comfort the afflicted, and afflict the comfortable."
This is the heart of the Christian gospel.

But there are those who have been poor,
    and those who have never been poor,
    who keep that openness,
    that awareness of their need for God,
        and for one another.

The comradeship, the mutual help, the little kindnesses,
    the caring and comfort that people give to each other
        in times of sadness or distress or illness
    become part of a whole attitude to life
        that is not spoiled by attaining some comfort and security.

We are nearing Lent,
    the season that challenges us to check our attitude toward life
        and those who need our riches.
May it be a time for us
    to become more open and aware of our need for God
        and for one another.
A poor woman once said, "The only real security is other people."

1 Sam 26:2, 7–9, 12–13, 22–23; 1 Cor 15:45–49; Luke 6:27–38

Imagine

"Be merciful, just as your Father is merciful." (Luke 6:36)

To be without mercy or compassion
    is to be cut off from the rest of the human race
    and from God.

Come away, O human child!
To the water, and the wild
With a faery, hand in hand.
For the world's more full of weeping
Than you can understand.
    —W.B. Yeats, "Stolen child"

Jesus calls upon us to put ourselves in the place of others;
    to ask ourselves, "What if it were you?"

Imagination is a capacity we all have.
With children, imagination is a magic toy.
It enables them
    to go anywhere, to be anybody, to do anything.
With the passing of time, they will outgrow childish games,
    but hopefully they will not forsake their magic toy.
They will never outgrow the need for it.

Look at Jesus.
Have you ever noticed the part imagination played in his life?
He pictured himself in the place of others,
    so much so that he could actually feel their pain.
"I was hungry and you gave me no food.
I was thirsty, and you gave me nothing to drink." (Matt 25:42)

That is a vivid use of imagination.

Jesus pictured himself in the place of others so clearly
    that their need became his need.
What happened to them happened to him.

A lively imagination is essential to great living.
The stories that Jesus told have hints of this same trait.

Do you remember the story about the rich man and Lazarus?
One lived in luxury
    and the other begged for the crumbs that fell from his table.

What was wrong with this rich man?
As far as we know, he was an honest and decent person.
But he had no imagination.

He saw Lazarus. That was inevitable.
He walked right past him everyday,
    but he never did allow himself to feel what Lazarus was feeling.

In essence, this is the story of a rich man
    who went to hell for want of an imagination.
He failed to put himself in the place of the poor beggar who lay at his gate.

This is the problem with some husbands and wives.
Both of them try to carry their part of the load.
He does his work and she does hers.
But, in a sense, they live in two different worlds.
Neither one ever looks at life through the eyes of the other.
Their marriage would be so much better
    if once in a while they could imagine what the other was feeling.
"I've looked at life from both sides now…."

We cannot be genuinely Christian without
the active use of our imagination.

Jesus came into a world of limited friendship.
And what did he do?
One of the first things he did was to teach people to say, "Our Father."

These two little words, more than anything else,
    have doomed the fences of the world.

If I say, "Our Father" and you say, "Our Father"
    that means we are brothers and sisters.
I am committed to you and you are committed to me.

To be Christian is to enlarge our appreciation of other people.
Try to imagine what it is like to be
    Black, Asian, Hispanic
    in a society that is dominated by Caucasians.

We may never know the answer to that question,
    but we cannot be followers of Christ
    and dare to say, "Our Father"
        unless we at least ask it.

There is one more word, and that is compassion.
It means to feel what someone else is feeling.
The ability to do that
    is probably the most divine dimension in a human heart.
It is one area where we are most like the Christ.
He not only knows our pain; he feels it as we feel it.
And he cannot deepen our sympathies until we are able to do the same.

But getting there can be
    and probably will be
    a very trying experience.

It certainly was for Jesus.
His incredible grip on the world is rooted in the reality that he speaks,
    not from an armchair but from a cross.
His entire life was hard.

Is it any wonder that he is able to feel our pain as if it were his own?

Now he calls us to do the same, to put ourselves in the place of others.

"Truly I tell you, just as you did it to one of the least of these
    who are members of my family,
    you did it to me." (Matt 25:40)

Sir 27:5–8; 1 Cor 15:54–58; Luke 6:39–45

A Holy Fool

Today's gospel is a lesson in eye care.
It is a much-needed lesson
    because we all are born with a film over our eyes.
Some never cleanse the lens so as to see for themselves.
They depend on seeing-eye people to interpret for them.

One who saw life clearly was the movie character, Forrest Gump.
    He spoke and acted from the heart always.

He may not have said what was socially acceptable
    or did what was politically correct.
But no one doubted his good intentions,
    and so he was attractive to people of all ages.
Most found him irresistible.

Forrest Gump was a kind of "contemporary holy fool,"
    just like St. Francis was and many other saints.
His I.Q. was below normal
    but his E.Q. (Emotional Quotient) was above average.

He learned and lived the philosophy of life
    his mother taught him,
        "Life is like a box of chocolates.
      You never know what you're gonna get."

Forrest had unconditional love for Jenny.
Forrest wanted to save Jenny,
    who through no fault of her own,
    experienced a dysfunctional childhood,
        but Jenny wouldn't let him.

God wants to save us
    when we are dysfunctional
        but often we won't let him.

Forrest's unconditional love
    for Lieutenant Don,
    who was on the edge of human and spiritual despair
    after losing both legs in the Vietnam war,
        might be a reminder
        of the unconditional love
        that we need to have for one another.

Only a "holy fool" displays this kind of love.
We all once had the child-like innocence of Forrest Gump,
    and we still have the capacity for it.
The problem is that often times
    it is covered by layer upon layer of conditioning
    that needs to be removed.

Our tendency is to operate more like Jenny than Forrest Gump,
    and we need to change that.
We need conversion.

Jenny says to Forrest at one point,
"You don't know what love is,"
    but she was wrong.

He says, "I'm not a smart man,
    but I know what love is."
He demonstrated it over and over again.

Finally, Jenny marries him,
    but we get the impression it was a case of
    "I need you; therefore I love you."
Where with Forrest it was
    "I love you; therefore I need you."

God needs us because he loves us.

He does not love us because he needs us.

The kind of love God wants to give us remains with us,
    helping us to grow,
as the second reading said,
    "Therefore my beloved, be steadfast, immovable,
        always excelling in the work of the Lord." (1 Cor 15:58)

Just like Forrest Gump.

When we focus on the kind of love Jenny was seeking,
    we discover that it really is not love.
That's one big problem with romantic love.
It often looks and feels like the real thing, but it is not.

The gospel today asks:
    "Why do you see the speck in your neighbor's eye,
        but do not notice the log in your own eye?" (Luke 6:41)
Despite the obvious splinters and logs in Lieutenant Dan's eyes,
    Forrest Gump did not even notice them.

In one scene when he noticed Lieutenant Dan on the dock,
    he was so glad to see him that he jumped off the boat
    and swam to the dock to greet him,
    even though there was nobody left on board to direct the boat!

Only a holy fool would do something like that,
    but this is a good image of the unconditional love God has for us.

Despite our many faults and shortcomings, God loves us,
    that is, if we will just show up
    and sincerely offer to be of assistance despite all our handicaps.
God will respond in a way that is always unbelievable.

God loves us more than we love God
    and much more than we love ourselves.

Forrest Gump did not need a course in theology.
He said, matter of factly, with a simple faith,
    "I'm going to heaven."
    and every person watching the movie,
        young and old, agreed.

During this week
    let's allow the Forrest Gump in all of us to come to the surface.
We need to be reminded of the simple unchanging truths about life.
"Life is like a box of chocolates.
    You never know what you are gonna get."

But you will have a lot of enjoyment trying to taste and experience as much of
life as you can with someone else,
    and that's one sweet life.

Zech 12:10–11, 13:1; Gal 3:26–29; Luke 9:18–24

Witnesses to Christ

The popularity of the John Gresham novels
    and TV series like "Law and Order" and "People's Court"
        demonstrates our appetite for stories involving the legal system.

The witness has a pivotal role in the drama.
The entire case usually revolves around the testimony of the witness.

In our gospel text today, Jesus calls us forward to be witnesses.
And like a good attorney, he prepares us in advance for the task.

What does it mean for us to be witnesses to Christ?
Here are some insights.

Witnesses need not be afraid to step forward.
The witness is not on trial.
Our Hebrew Testament reminds us of this fact, too.
Jeremiah did not need to be afraid.
The world was the one on trial, not Jeremiah.
The witnesses need to remember that they are not the ones being tried.

Christ calls us forward as witnesses.
He tells us the task will not be easy
    or always well received by those to whom we bear witness.
But he assures us that he will be with us.

Do not be afraid of the cross-examination of the world.
Witnesses do not have to bear the burden of convincing the jury.
The witness simply tells the truth as he or she knows it.
Whether the jury or judge finds the testimony compelling
    is not the burden the witness must bear.

If we think we must convince, we will try too hard.
We will be too forceful.
This is not faithful witnessing.

When you witness for Christ, just tell the truth as you know it.
Whether your witness is received or rejected
    is not your burden.
Many Christian witnesses forget this.

Let God deal with the ones to whom you bear witness.
God already cares for them.
You may be only one of a hundred gentle nudges that
    God means to place in their path.

Witnesses do not fabricate or embellish facts.
They tell the truth of their own experience.

In the courtroom drama,
    witnesses are not required,
    nor even allowed, to speak about the case
    beyond their own experience.
Objection; sustained; overruled.

The witness only tells his or her story.
It is the most powerful evidence anyone can bring.

When you bear witness for Christ,
    just speak or act out of your own experience.
You have no more powerful argument than your own life story.

Your experience is compelling for you.
That will be the source of your passion.
And your passion is more compelling than carefully chosen words.

You cannot hide your passion for Christ,
    even if you wanted to.
And why hide it?

Always remember,
the most effective witness to Christ is often not words but action.
As Francis of Assisi taught his followers:
"Preach the gospel and if necessary use words."

So here is the truth.
God loves the entire world.
If you have experienced this love through Jesus Christ,
    just tell the truth,
    the whole truth,
    and nothing but the truth,
    so help you, God.

Today's gospel demands that we think about the strength of our own faith.
We need to consider more than our Sunday best.
We must also face our Wednesday worst!
Will we always acknowledge Jesus before others,
    or by our silence will we disown him?

Priests and teachers go through a long period of training
    to earn the right to speak on behalf of the Church.
But each of us can be a Christian witness
    without attending a seminary or earning a degree in theology.
We can bear witness to our faith
    by simply telling the story of our lives.

It is the truth that we know.

1 Kings 19:16b, 19–21; Gal 5:1, 13–18; Luke 9:51–62

"Cat's in the Cradle"

Will Rogers, the great American humorist, was part Native American.

One day a woman was boasting
    that her ancestors came over on the Mayflower.
After she had finished her ego trip,
    she turned to Rogers and said,
    "What about your ancestors?"
Rogers glanced at the floor, shuffled his feet and said,
    "My ancestors met the Mayflower."

(It's good that Jesus didn't marry and raise a family.
It saves a lot of people
    the trouble of trying to trace their ancestry back to him.)

A six-year-old child's parents took him to visit the Mayflower.
As soon as they got on board,
    the child began talking away merrily
    to the well-dressed mannequin who greeted them.
The statue wore a beautiful print dress,
    white apron, and a black hat with a bow tie.

It looked very real to the child
    and so he told the mannequin the whole story of his trip.
He didn't realize the mistake he was making
    until half a boat load of tourists were standing around him, laughing.

To say he was embarrassed is to minimize how he felt.
He was mortified,
    and that is why he walked up to the next supposed mannequin,
    dressed the same way, and kicked her right in the shins—hard.

But that second mannequin was a real human being.
Discovering the difference between the real and the phony
    is not a task just for six-year-olds.

The disciples lived with a Jesus
    they didn't really know or believe in.

They watched him closely;
    they witnessed his signs and wonders
    and the first chance they got,
    they went after a village of poor Samaritans
     and wanted them destroyed.

James and John asked,
    "Lord, do you want us to command fire
    to come down from heaven and consume them?" (Luke 9:53–55)

Jesus is very much like the second mannequin,
    the one who got kicked.
In the real story, the child stayed mad; his foot hurt.
He didn't like being fooled.
But if Jesus was the mannequin who got kicked
    because the little boy was humiliated, sad, and hurt,
I would like to believe that Jesus would have found him later.

He would have rubbed his own shin, still hurting,
    and put his arm around the child and said something like this,
"It's okay. Lots of people make the same mistake."
He would continue,
    "They mistake the phony for the real. Don't worry about it.
    Let's go look at the rest of the boat together."

What makes our Messiah real?
    His stripes, his wounds, his bruised skin?

No, not just these.

What makes our Messiah real
  is that he overcomes hurt,
  is raised from the dead,
  and he comes back to us.
He forgives us for not trusting him,
  especially when we put things off, procrastinate.

Just for a moment take another look at today's gospel.

Did you notice how many times the expressions
"Let me" and "then" occur?

In the first reading, when Elijah asks Elisha to follow him, Elisha replies,
"Let me kiss my father and my mother and then I will follow you."

In the gospel, when Jesus extends a similar invitation, one man responds,
"Let me first go bury my father." (Luke 9:59)

This seems to be a legitimate excuse
  and Jesus' response comes as a shock to our ears.
In effect, Jesus was saying that those
  who do not share the new life he was offering
  were in effect "dead."

Jesus said, "No one who puts a hand to the plow
  and looks back is fit for the kingdom of God." (Luke 9:61)

Often when we catch ourselves using the expression "Let me,"
  it is a way to delay decision and commitment.

For example:
  let me enjoy this piece of cake and then I'll diet.
  let me complete this work and then I will pray.
  let us buy a bigger house and then we we'll have a baby.

We can sound convincing, but when we procrastinate, it's often too late.
  Food becomes an addiction;

and prayer has become a foreign language.
   The pregnancy is no longer possible.
This is very well said in a song called
"Cat's in the Cradle" by Harry Chapin.

A father misses his son's birth and boyhood
   because he's too busy with other things.
   Inadvertently he passes on this same habit,
   this same destructive tendency to his son.
In the future the child will probably also inherit
   his father's loneliness, doubt, and late moment of truth.

Let's listen to "Cat's in the Cradle" by Harry Chapin.

My child arrived just the other day.
He came to the world in the usual way.
But there were planes to catch and bills to pay.
He learned to walk while I was away.
And he was talking 'fore I knew it, and as he grew
He'd say, "I'm gonna be like you, Dad.
You know I'm gonna be like you."

   And the cat's in the cradle and the silver spoon
   Little boy blue and the man on the moon.
   "When you comin' home dad?"
   "I don't know when, but we'll get together then, son,
   You know we'll have a good time then."

My son turned ten just the other day.
He said. "Thanks for the ball, Dad. Come on, let's play.
Can you teach me to throw?"
I said, "Not today. I got a lot to do."
He said, "That's okay,"
And he walked away, but his smile never dimmed.
And said, "I'm gonna be like him, yeah,
You know I'm gonna be like him."

Well he came from college just the other day.
So much like a man, I just had to say,
"Son, I'm proud of you. Can you sit for awhile?"
He shook his head and said with a smile.
"What I'd really like dad, is to borrow the car keys.
See you later. Can I have them please?"

I've long since retired. My son's moved away.
I called him up just the other day.
I said, "I'd like to see you if you don't mind."
He said, "I'd love to, Dad, if I can find the time.
You see, my new job's a hassle and the kids have the flu.
But it's sure nice talking to you, Dad.
It's been sure nice talking to you."

And as I hung up the phone it occurred to me...
He'd grown up just like me.
My boy was just like me.

We do not always carry out our good intentions.
We procrastinate.

The Lord will forgives us for not trusting in him and letting others down.
However, let us ask the Holy Spirit
    to enlighten us in the decisions we must make in our lives
        during the prayers of the faithful today.

Let this be our prayer.

O Lord, free us from our procrastination.
Give us the courage to stand firm and carry out our good intentions.
Let us follow you
    and love others without reservation. Amen.

A Glimpse of Fr. Hayes

Fr. Hayes and Holmes, his cat, spent many contemplative hours together in the rectory. Here is one of his favorite poems, "Pangur Ban."

I and Pangur Ban, my cat
  'Tis a like task we are at:
  Hunting mice is his delight
  Hunting words I sit all night.

Better far than praise of men
  'Tis to sit with book and pen;
  Pangur bears me no ill-will,
  He too plies his simple skill.

Tis a merry task to see
  At our tasks how glad are we,
  When at home we sit and find
  Entertainment to our mind.

Oftentimes a mouse will stray
  In the hero Pangur's way;
  Oftentimes my keen thought set
  Takes a meaning in its net.

'Gainst the wall he sets his eye
    Full and fierce and sharp and sly;
    'Gainst the wall of knowledge I
    All my little wisdom try.

When a mouse darts from its den,
    O how glad is Pangur then!
    O what joy comes from above
    When I solve the doubts I love!

So in peace our task we ply,
    Pangur Ban, my cat, and I;
    In our arts we find our bliss,
    I have mine and he has his.

Practice every day has made
    Pangur perfect in his trade;
    I get wisdom day and night
    Turning darkness into light.

—Written by an unknown monk in the ninth century
and translated by Robin Flower

Isa 66:10–14c; Gal 6:14–18; Luke 10:1–12, 17–20

Pairs

It is easier for a non-Christian to become a Christian
    than it is for someone who is a Christian
        to become a Christian.

Jesus was faced with a labor shortage.
He had more to do than he could possibly get done by himself.
To help alleviate the situation,
    he chose twelve associates whom he called apostles.

If the twelve apostles were sent to the lost sheep of the tribe of Israel,
    the seventy in today's gospel have an even broader mission.
They are to announce the coming of the kingdom not only to Jews,
but to Samaritans and Gentiles as well.
In Christ's time,
it was popularly believed that there were seventy nations in the world.
Thus Jesus' seventy disciples symbolized the universal mission
    to evangelize all the nations;
    all the outsiders were now invited to be insiders.

Once that was done, Jesus said, "The harvest is rich,
but the laborers are few."
He was still short-handed.

Part of the assignment given to the seventy was to pray for more workers.

Then he sent them out in pairs.
Given the labor shortage, why cut your labor force in half?
An efficiency expert
    would have probably recommended a different approach.

Send them out individually.
Then they can cover twice as much territory,
see twice as many people, and virtually double their production.

When more help was so badly needed,
 why did Jesus send them out in pairs?

I think it was because Jesus knew that life is essentially a partnership.
In order to be our best selves, and do our best work,
 we must have the involvement of at least one other person.
We need partnerships to make life rich.

I mean rich in quality, rich in faith, rich in knowledge,
 rich in wisdom, and rich in hope.

I cannot generate these qualities all by myself.
I need your help.
The only way I can become a loving person
 is for you to love me and allow me to love you in return.
The only way I can resolve conflict
 is for you and me to have a disagreement,
 work through it, and remain friends.
Most of hope has come from people who remained hopeful
 when they seemed to have every reason for giving up.

Jesus sent those seventy disciples out to do something.
They were also sent to become something.

They were all newcomers to the Christian faith.
They had to be.
The movement itself was just getting under way.
There was no such thing as a Church
 or the *Catechism of the Catholic Church* to guide them.
There was not even a new Testament.

Novate nobis novale
Et nolite serere super spinas

"Break up your fallow ground, and do not sow among thorns." (Jeremiah 4:3)

They were preaching the gospel and learning to practice it at the same time.
To do that and do it well, they needed someone by their side.

Their faith would be put to the test
    and it surely helped to have someone along who shared that faith.
Jesus gave each of those disciples
    someone with whom they could practice that fine art.

We need partnerships for the enrichment of life and our faith.
We need partnerships to give life stability.

Two people walking the same road
    can borrow that from one another.
The people who depend on us give us roots.
They keep us from giving up and running away.
They keep us at the task when we are tempted to quit.

A popular song from a few years ago put it this way:
    "Lean on me when you are not strong.
    I'll be your friend;
    I'll help you carry on."

The people in today's gospel could have sung that song to one another.
Everyone of them had somebody to lean on:
    "the seventy returned in jubilation."

They were celebrating.
The mission adventure was over.
It was a wonderful success.
All the way home, they had someone with whom to rejoice.

No one understood that better than Jesus
    as he sent his disciples out two by two.

Deut 30:10–14; Col 1:15–20; Luke 10:25–37

Too Heavenly-Minded?

Statistics tell us that most Catholics come to Mass to feel close to God.
It has been said that statistics don't lie,
    but interpreters do differ.

Do we come to church on Sunday
    "to fill up on God"
      —to fill up our spiritual tanks
    to get through the rest of the week?

Do we come to escape the absurdity of our daily world
    to find a heavenly world
        with our own tranquility base?

When the very first Soviet cosmonauts came back to earth,
    they declared that they hadn't seen God in the heavens.
It was a silly commentary,
    but there is a sense in which they were correct.

Often even religious people have a static view of God.
God is in another world
    up there,
and only by very special means
        can we ever come close to God.

For some, God is only found in the Bible
    or in the Eucharist
    or in some secret formula for which you have to bargain.

In today's Scriptures, two people struggle
    with the question of God's place in our world.

In the first reading, Moses tells his people
    not to look for the meaning of God
        in something mysterious and remote.

God's commandments are no longer written on tablets of stone,
    but are engraved on the heart.
Moses says God's law "is very near to you;
    it is in your mouth and in your heart for you to observe." (Deut 30:14)

In the gospel today, the lawyer is a believer.
He believes in God and knows his "catechism."
He knows that the law says,
 "You shall love the Lord your God with all your heart
    and with all your soul,
    and with all your strength,
    and with all your mind;
    and your neighbor as yourself." (Luke 10:27)

But the business of lawyers is precision.
They must always be sure of definitions
    and so he asks,
    "Who is my neighbor?"

No matter how we try,
we can never get the full shock of Jesus' answer.
His parable of the Good Samaritan
    blows the sandals off his listener's feet.

For the Jews,
    Samaritans were radically impure,
    politically dangerous,
    and religiously heretical.

I heard recently about a postal worker
    who didn't want to handle the letters of people with AIDS.
He was afraid he would get the virus
    because the AIDS people had licked and sealed the envelope.

For generations the Jews had been told,
    even by their great prophets like Hosea and Ezekiel,
    that the Samaritans were definitely not neighbors.

The priest and the Levite pass by the man in the ditch.
It's easy to stereotype these two religious leaders.
The priest and Levite probably were moved by the pitiful victim.
No doubt they stopped to look
    and almost became
    the good priest and the good Levite.
But something kept them from doing the human thing.
It was the law.

The story says that the man was "half dead."

The priest and the Levite,
    despite their feelings of pity,
        were bound by the law which said
        they would be virtually impure if they touched a corpse.

The law won out over the law engraved on their hearts.

Heaven clashed with earth and heaven won.
They were "so heavenly-minded; they were no earthly-good."

The Samaritan is "moved to pity."
He proves to be the neighbor. Why?
    Because he acts like a neighbor.
The Samaritan's heavenly world,
    his religious world,
    pays attention to his daily world.
His God is not in the sky,
    but very near.

I think the story of the Good Samaritan
    gives us insight into our question
    of why we come to Mass on Sunday.

The desire to feel closer to God
   is one of the most human desires of our hearts.

But the true goal of our Sunday worship
   in Word and sacrament,
   is to make us aware
      that God is not just in church, but in our lives.

God's grace is not locked up in a church building,
   or found only in a Bible,
   or a tabernacle,
   or in a homily.

God's grace is in the world,
   especially in those times and events
      when we seem empty or at our wit's end.

God's grace is found when our journey to Jericho
   is interrupted by unexpected or strange demands.

Grace is found when we are moved to change direction
   and our plans
      to help another person in need.

We come to church on Sunday
   as a believing community,
      not simply to "get grace,"
but rather to celebrate a world full of grace
      and a God who is very near.

"Samaritans are a funny breed
They try to help people in need
Give time and labor
To be a good neighbor
No thank you notes required."

Gen 18:1–10a; Col 1:24–28; Luke 10:38–42

Mary and the Happy Hour

Mary or Martha, which one was the Good Samaritan to Jesus?

There have always been a variety of interpretations
    of Luke's story of Mary, Martha, and Jesus,
        and they continue to this day.
Some interpretations
    portray Martha embracing the active life
    and Mary practicing the contemplative life.

A modern interpretation suggests the story
    represents the conflicts and concerns
        that women have about what should be their priorities,
        the career world or the home world.

The usual preachers give the back of the hand to Martha,
    and doesn't the text seem to agree?

Doesn't Jesus seem to rebuke the busy housewife,
    whose meal he will shortly enjoy?

You will never get the cooks and the hostesses
    to be happy about this gospel,
    which certainly appears to be unfair
        in its lack of appreciation
        for the labor involved with preparing a meal!

Yes, it's unfair, like so many other stories Jesus tells,
    which by any human measure are puzzling.
For example, it was unfair to pay a full day's wage to those workers
    who came at the end of the day.

God does operate by a different measure
and often the ways of God are mysterious to us.

But one thing is required if we are to see the meaning of things in this story:
What good is action if we are all action;
if we never find time
for rest, reflection, and paying attention to others and ourselves?

Few things make a visitor more welcome
than someone who is eager to listen.
That is the part Mary was playing.
She was a good listener.
But this comfortable arrangement did not last long.
At some point Martha came back into the room all bent out of shape,
and interestingly enough took her frustration out on Jesus.

"Lord, do you not care
that my sister has left me to do all the work by myself?
Tell her then to help me." (Luke 10:40)

But Jesus refused to do that.
He sided with Mary and gently rebuked Martha.

He answered her, "Martha, Martha,
you are worried and distracted by many things.
There is need of only one thing.
Mary has chosen the better part,
which will not be taken away from her." (Luke 10:41–42)

What happened after that we are not told.
Did the meal ever get cooked?
But suppose it did.
Do you think Jesus would really have enjoyed it?
Could you enjoy a meal served by a self-proclaimed martyr?

"Well, here it is.
I hope you enjoy it.
I nearly killed myself getting it ready for you."

Jesus had visited there many times
    and nothing like this had happened before.
This would spoil the taste of the finest feast.

The reason may lie in the timing of the visit.
The writer of Luke places this story in the gospel
    right after the story of the Good Samaritan
        in which we are taught to get busy, to take action.

We all know that there is a lot to commend Martha
    for her response to a perceived need.
    It was similar to the response of the Good Samaritan to the half-dead man.
But there is a difference in the circumstances.
While Martha was attempting to offer the best service she could to Jesus,
    it is crucial that she distinguish
        between what Jesus actually needed
        and what she was offering him.

If we follow the chronology of Luke's account,
    we see that Jesus' experience
        in the home of Mary and Martha in Bethany
        was while he was on his way to Jerusalem,
        where he would encounter his final conflict
            with the religious and political power structures.

Now, in the hospitality of Martha's home,
    Jesus was seeking refuge and respite
        from the demands of the huge crowds
        who followed him day after day.

This was a day to be "off duty,"
    away from the constant spotlight of controversy and danger.

Jesus apparently sought in their home
   a place where he could be free of these demands.
In this secure environment,
   he might "re-create" after his demanding schedule
      of preaching, teaching, healing,
      and debate with those who tried to subvert his message and appeal.

His longings and his expectations
   were not matched by Martha's reaction to him.

 She thought it was her duty to make a fuss,
   and became distracted from her visitor
      by involvement in the preparation of a meal.
All he wanted was her presence and companionship.

Martha gave her best,
   but what she offered was not what he needed.
There is an English proverb:
   "It is a sin against hospitality to open your doors
      and shut up your countenance."

Yet, it is all too easy to identify with Martha's reaction.

Jesus gently said,
"Martha, Martha, you are worried and distracted by many things;
   there is need of only one thing.
Mary has chosen the better part,
   which will not be taken away from her." (Luke 10:41–42)

The better part was that Mary had become Jesus' partner in conversation,
   the one who shared his thoughts and ideas.
It is the model for ways in which women
   are continuing to contribute to the dialogue
      and decisions in the Church.

Jesus asks her, and us, very directly, to get our priorities right.
Jesus is saying to Martha, and to us,
    to allow ourselves to be loved for ourselves
        and not for what we do
          to justify our existence.

The love that we seek is not dependent
    on our looks accomplishments, gifts, talents, or abilities.
We have to allow ourselves to be
    and to be in touch with Jesus
    who re-creates us and makes us whole.

Today we are asked to realize that being all action is not enough.
    Something we see in Mary
    teaches us to take time to listen
    and be in the presence of Jesus,
    to have a happy hour with him.

A Glimpse of Fr. Hayes

On a warm summer night around 2:30 a.m., I heard voices right outside our open bedroom window. Startled, I woke my husband, Chuck, who immediately got up and got dressed. Shortly after, the doorbell rang, and there was Fr. Mike and a man who had lived in Carlton years ago.

Fr. Mike told us that he had a bet with this man that he could wake up his friends in the middle of the night, and that they wouldn't be mad. Well, we weren't mad and even made breakfast for them. Fr. Mike's friend also knew my dad, who lived just across the road and he went over to see Dad and to catch a ride back into Carlton.

About 7:30 AM, as Chuck and I were getting ready to go to work, Fr. Mike climbed into our bed to get some sleep. As we were going out the door, he hollered out… "Chuck, wake me up at 11:00, as I have Mass today at noon!" I'm glad someone got some sleep.

—Jean Johnson, former parishioner of St. Francis, Carlton, MN

Gen 18:20–32; Col 2:12–14; Luke 11:1–13

"Da," Our Father

"What we ought to pray for
   is in the Lord's Prayer.
What is not in it,
   we ought not to pray for."
—St. Augustine

There is an old story told of St. Benedict.
   He was traveling on a long journey by horseback
      and he met a beggar along the road.
The beggar recognized Benedict and sneered at him.
"Isn't it a fine thing to be a man of prayer,
   and to own a horse as well."
Benedict, being a man of the gospel, replied,
 "My friend, if you can say the Lord's prayer
   without being distracted,
   I will make you a present of the horse."

The beggar could hardly believe his luck,
   and so immediately began:
"Our Father, who art in heaven, hallowed be thy name,
   thy kingdom come, thy will be done
      on earth as it is in heaven.
Give us this day our daily bread…
   and then he paused, looked up at Benedict and asked,
   "Does that include the saddle and bridle as well?"

Scripture scholars agree that the core of Jesus' being
   was an unshakable sense of God as his personal Father.

Scripture itself says that Jesus was like us in all unsinful things,
  and that he grew in wisdom and grace.
So we may presume that he learned to pray as we do,
  one step at a time.

Jesus began life like the rest of us,
  crawling around the floor, babbling nonsense syllables.
Now some syllables roll off the tongue more easily than others,
  and after a little babbling, all of us stumble onto
    da…da…dada.

Of course, we don't know what we are saying,
  but it makes Dad proud.

So Jesus crawled around the dirt floor of his home
  and in his own Aramaic language tripped across ah…ah…ba…abba.
He didn't know what he was saying either,
  but I believe it made his Father very proud.

The next step that all of us take is to say other people's prayers.
So Jesus learned his people's prayer, like this beautiful psalm:
"Lord, you know me when I sit down and when I rise up…,
  you knit me in my mother's womb."

But even after he learned what each word meant,
  he could not have incorporated such adult sentiment
    into his childhood experience of life.

The next time we meet Jesus is when he is lost and found in the temple.
His mother scolded,
"Look, your Father and I have been searching for you in great anxiety."
  (Luke 2: 48)
And Jesus innocently replied,
  "Did you not know that I must be in my Father's house?"

The very first words of Jesus recorded in the Gospel of Luke, were
    "My Father's house."
His very last words were,
    "Father, into your hands I commend my spirit." (Luke 23:46)

The gospel of Luke tells us that Mary did not understand what he meant.
Could it also be true
    that neither did Jesus know entirely what he was saying?

Did he wonder?
Did he think, "I wonder why I said that?
What is happening to me
    that I feel, but don't quite understand?"

Scripture says that Mary pondered these things in her heart,
    and we may presume that Jesus did the same
        as he went back home with them
        to grow in wisdom and grace.

As we mature, other people's prayers begin to make more sense.
We experience similar things,
    so their prayer becomes our prayer.

But we and Jesus have unique experiences
    that no one else has ever had or will have.
And when we talk with God about them,
    our prayer becomes unique, one of a kind.

Jesus so shaped his life around God
    that his life took another leap of faith around the age of thirty.
Although he loved his parents,
    he began to feel uncomfortable, restless, somehow unfulfilled.

Something was not altogether as it should be.
So he left his mother and father and his childhood home
    in a wandering search for the answers.

He fell in with some other seekers of truth,
    and one day decided to be baptized.
When he emerged from the water, a voice declared,
"You are my Son, the Beloved;
    with you I am well pleased." (Luke 3:22)

Suddenly, the whole life of Jesus passed in review and fell into focus.

He realized that saying "abba" at eight months was not just baby talk;
    that calling the temple his "Father's house" at age twelve
        was not just confusion.

The fact crashed in on Jesus
    that the Lord of heaven and earth was his own personal Father.

That discovery was his guiding star from that moment on.
Whether he ate, worked, slept, or prayed,
    the breath of the Father was on his face.
The will of his Father was his meat and drink, his very life.

He always did what his Father wanted.
If he wasn't quite sure what that was,
    he would sneak away to pray in search of that will.
The preoccupation with his Father never left him.

It was never enough for Jesus,
    nor is it ever enough for us, to pray other people's prayers.
We have to create a private language,
    to talk about our unique life-in-God.

When we talk to God as Jesus has taught us,
    we are drawn into his relationship with God
        and with all whom he has embraced and loved.
If not, our prayer is merely lip-service.
Today's gospel leaves an unanswered question.
Which of the disciples said,
    "Lord, teach us to pray?"

Was it Peter, James, John, or Andrew?
We don't know.

Maybe that space was left blank for a purpose,
    written that way so each of us can fill in his or her name.

It would read like this:
"One of his disciples (your name) said.
'Lord, teach us.
    I am ready to learn.
    My mind is open and receptive.'"
And the Master teacher will take it from there.

A Glimpse of Fr. Hayes

I was playing golf at the Moose Lake golf course, and Fr. Mike was a hole or two ahead of me. As I was walking toward hole number three, which Fr. Mike had just played, a golf club fell out of a tree. It was an old club, so you can guess who I thought it belonged to. When asked though, Fr. Mike said it must have been an act of God since he would never throw a golf club like that.

   I have yet to determine the accuracy of his statement and so will have to wait, hopefully for many years, to receive further clarification on the matter. Fr. Mike was an excellent golfer and he proved that the clubs did not make the golfer; rather, it was a result of personal skill.

—John Hanson, summer resident of Moose Lake, MN

Eccl 1:2, 2:21–23; Col 3:1–5, 9–11; Luke 12:13–21

Enjoying God's Gifts

Jesus didn't teach us to pray
   "Give us this day ten times our daily bread."

Today Jesus gathers us to himself
   and speaks words that are not easy to hear.
Let us be open and vulnerable
   to the challenges today's gospel sets forth.

Here's a story for you…

There is an eight-minute French cartoon
   about an empty village and a stranger who enters the deserted town.
Where are the people?
All the signs of life are there,
   nothing is locked,
   food is on the table,
   smoke is curling in the chimneys,
   stores are open but empty of customers.
He doesn't understand, but he proceeds to have a wonderful time.
Soon he is too drunk and happy
   to realize that the villagers are all on a nearby hill
   and are desperately trying to signal to him.
They had rushed outside the town
   because they were told
   that a huge bomb in the town square was about to go off.
They left everything to save their lives.

From a safe distance,
   they try vainly by gestures and shouting to warn the stranger,
      taking care not to come too close.

They watch him eat their food,
   drink their liquor, and try on their clothes.

But when the happy wanderer goes into the bank
   and flings their money up into the air,
   they forget everything but their greed.
They rush back to the village,
   beat up the stranger, and drive him out.
At that moment the bomb explodes.
They all die, except the stranger.

Let's examine the issue of greed
   because it is important enough for Jesus
      to tell a parable about it in today's gospel.

Greed: You need more than three drawers for your socks.
Enjoying gifts from God:
   You like your socks clean and prefer them without holes.

Greed: Your car needs to be a current model,
   loaded with every option and with vanity plates.
Enjoying gifts from God:
   You would prefer that your car start,
   and not leave too much oil on the driveway.

Greed: Your clothes must have the right label.
Enjoying gifts of God:
   You have a warm sweater.

Greed: You have every CD ever made.
Enjoying gifts from God:
   You have a collection of CDs
   that you try to keep in the right cases.

How many times have we heard about those
    who win the lottery,
        or become professional athletes,
    or inherit great wealth,
    only to discover that their relationships
        and spirits become crushed
            under the weight of their newly found gain?

We think we would be different
    if we came into such wealth,
    but are we sure?

How many of us have learned
    not to hug that which cannot hug us back?

The epitaph of our society may be
"They loved things, and used people."
But the point of life is to learn instead
"to love people and use things."

How will we learn this?

We learn this by modeling our lives,
    not on the pattern of the rich farmer,
    but on the life of the one who told us the story of the rich farmer.
His hope was that we would find the true wealth of life.

The story of the rich fool is found in many places,
    but Jesus tells it so well.
He ends with a great punch line about growing rich in the sight of God.

"You fool!
This very night your life is being demanded of you.
    And the things you have prepared, whose will they be?
So it is with those who store up treasures for themselves
    but are not rich toward God." (Luke 12:20–21)

Wis 18:6–9; Heb 11:1–2, 8–19; Luke 12:32–48 or 12:35–40

To Hear with the Heart

Since it is faith that has gathered this praying assembly together today,
    from so many different places,
        and from so many varying histories and backgrounds…
Since it is faith that sustains each of us in our day-to-day activities
    from one week to the next.
Since it is faith that forms
    and transforms our relationships with Christ and with one another…
Since it is faith that will see us through every joy and sorrow,
    through all our successes and failures,
    and through every experience of light and darkness in our lives…
    it is truly appropriate that faith is the focus of this week's liturgy.

An African missionary was translating John's gospel into Songhai.
When the missionary couldn't find a word to translate "to believe,"
    he asked a native African how to translate it.

The native thought momentarily and said,
    "I think 'to believe' should be translated 'to hear with the heart.'"

But hearing with our heart means responding with our heart, too.
Faith is also a verb.
It calls us to "be dressed for action and have [our] lamps lit." (Luke 12:35)

In our modern images, "dressed for action with our lamps lit,"
    might make you think of firefighters or rescue crews ready to go.
But a mother of a sick child,
    half asleep in the dark,
    instantly responding to the cry of her child,
    is equally alert and ready for action.
She has heard her child's cry with her heart.

Jesus' image is one of attitude.
Jesus expects us to be so alert in faith
    that we see what is needed,
    and when we see,
    we act.

To be a follower of Jesus is to be the one who serves,
    even if the need arises inconveniently,
        at midnight or at dawn.

A teacher at a Catholic university begins each freshman class
    by asking students to write out a short biography.
One of the questions, which surprises them a little is,
"Have you been part of any service organization up to now?"

He explains he is not recruiting,
    but preparing them to understand the gospels.
In a course in Christianity,
    they will discover that it is not just a matter of believing
    but of doing.
What they are called to do is works of service.

The students come up with a surprising number of things
    they already participate in
    such as working with disadvantaged children, tutoring,
    participating in Big Brother, Big Sister programs.
One was part of a clown ministry that visited nursing homes.
Several had worked for Habitat for Humanity,
    just as the former president Jimmy Carter and his wife, Rosalynn, do.
This famous couple gives a month each year
    to this apostolate of the hammer.

The world is a messy place,
    but this is where we are expected to bring about the reign of God
    that Jesus speaks of today.

The kingdom doesn't fall from heaven.

The reign of God or godly values,
    such as love, goodness, peace, and justice
    appear only when we have faith
        that listens "with the heart,"
    and we enter into a new relationship with our neighbor and our world.

The gospel stresses that we are gifted
    and the more gifted we are,
    the more obligated we are to service.

"From everyone to whom much has been given,
    much will be required." (Luke 12:48)

I recently read about an extraordinary example of service
    given by three Maryknoll sisters in Nicaragua.
They serve the needs of the poorest of the people,
    and they do it in ways that encourage the people to help themselves.
Handouts do not work for long,
    so the sisters developed what they call pastoral committees.

Because priests are scarce,
    the committees take on the responsibility
    of teaching catechism in the villages,
        preparing the liturgy,
        visiting the sick,
        caring for the church property,
        and often leading Sunday worship.

But then they engage in social and economic projects,
    which are essential in a region without adequate water or electricity.

They are building a communal oven to bake bread,
    beginning a sewing workshop,
    and organizing a brick-making factory.

They have built day schools,
    and if they get electricity,
    they will begin adult education at night.

Much of the aid the committees received in the past
    from the top down was siphoned off
    and did not produce a stable society.
They have to do it themselves, and they do,
    with the aid of these extraordinary nuns,
    supported by a network of interested people in the U.S. and Europe.

These aren't your "Sister Act" nuns;
    they genuinely live out the gospel.

We are called to do the same with our lives,
    with our gifts, talents, and blessings.
If we share these,
    and commit ourselves in one way or another to the works of service,
    we will be fulfilling the gospel, too.
We will be putting our faith into action;
    we will be hearing the call to faith and service with our heart.

How is God calling you to be "dressed for action with your lamp lit" today?
Maybe your light has been a bit dim lately.
Perhaps God is gently nudging you to listen with your heart,
    to act and to serve in a new way
    and with a new attitude.

Jer 38:4–6; Heb 12:1–4; Luke 12:49–53

Bring Fire to the Earth

"I came to bring fire to the earth,
     and how I wish it were already kindled!" (Luke 12:49)

Each one of us has a baptism
     with which we must be baptized,
     and through us
          God will cast the purifying fire
          of his love upon the earth.

In the gospel today, Jesus makes it quite clear
     that following him will bring us into tension,
          and conflict with the world around us.
The Christian message will bring us into conflict,
     as individuals and as a community,
     with a society that does not understand
     or even rejects,
          what we have to say.

There are any number of possible reactions to this.

The first one is to bury the problems
     or to hope that they will go away.
However, tension and conflict,
     as difficult as they may be to live with,
     are not exclusively negative realities.

The opposite of love is not hatred; it is indifference.

Jesus predicted that the Christian message
would arouse anger and division.
because he knew that when it is preached
and lived with conviction,
people cannot remain neutral.

We all lament the negative press,
the adverse comments
to which the Church is subjected at times,
but we can interpret them also as signs of hope.

They tell us that what we have to say
has not met with indifference.

They tell us that our lives
and our faith
have something to say to the world we live in.

Following Jesus
is to light a fire on the earth,
the fire of Christian faith.

Jesus wants us to ignite our own fire of faith.
He wants us to burn brightly for all to see.

He wants us to light up the darkness
right here in the places where we live,
our homes
and our workplaces,
our community
and our Church.

Isa 66:18–21; Heb 12:5–7, 11–13; Luke 13:22–30

Narrow Door or Wide Gate?

"Lord, will only a few be saved?" (Luke 13:23)
St. Augustine, an early theologian, would have answered "Yes."
Notice, Jesus did not answer the question.
Instead he said, "Strive to enter through the narrow door." (Luke 13:24)

Some of us assume, almost automatically,
  that he was talking about heaven,
    that he was telling people to struggle,
    to work,
    to discipline,
    their way into heaven.

I don't think so.
Heaven is entered through the wide gate of God's mercy.
We can leave that up to God.

Our problem is here and now.
A salvation that does some good
  is more concerned with getting us into life
    than into heaven.

Jesus ignored the question,
"Lord, will only a few be saved?" (Luke 13:23)
  and talked about a salvation that does some good.

We sit here today,
  a respectable congregation, with most of our needs met.
We have food to eat,
  clothes to wear,
  and houses in which to live.

I suppose we could sit here and convince ourselves
    that some day we will go to heaven.

Suppose that is true, and some day it will happen.
What difference would that make
    when so many of God's people are hungry, lonely, and cold?

How could we long for such assurance?
That would be nothing more than an expression of the same old problem.
We are more concerned with ourselves than we are for anyone else.
That is the very thing from which we need to be saved.
That is what Jesus came to save us from.

Jesus did not come to get us into heaven.
He came to get heaven into us.

I am not saying that the desire to go to heaven is unworthy.
But neither is it necessarily a virtue.
Some people want to go to heaven
    for the same reasons they want to move to a retirement village:
        the climate is good and the living is easy.

That kind of salvation does no good at all.
It only appeals to selfishness.

We need Christ to save us from specific and concrete sins.
I need him to correct all that is wrong in me.
You need him to correct all that is wrong in you.
And the two, added together,
    will surely make a difference to those who have to live with us.

A salvation that does some good requires effort.
Every worthwhile achievement in life is reached by a narrow door.
This means giving of ourselves, even as Christ has given himself to us.
Our selfishness, however, is deeply rooted;
    it will not die easily.

That is why Jesus says,
  "I tell you, many will try to enter and not be able." (Luke 13:24)

We could criticize the people in those ancient towns and villages
  for letting their chance pass them by, but we do the same thing.
Every one of us lets some of the golden opportunities of life slide by,
  unclaimed.
We could learn more,
  love more, sense more,
    give more, live more.
The possibilities of life are almost unlimited.

How do we miss them?
Where do they go?

I think most of the time we miss them through neglect.
That's what happened to the people in today's gospel.
They waited until the door of opportunity was already closed,
  and then they tried to enter.

That can happen to us and often does.
The opportunities of life come and go;
    they don't wait around forever.
That is why we should live each day to the fullest.
Don't let the possibilities of this day go unclaimed;
  they are much too valuable to throw away.

Those who are saved
  and will be saved
  are those who are busy about the things of God:
    mercy, joy, truth, compassion, and justice.

Those who are saved and will be saved
  are trying to bring a little bit of heaven down to earth now.
This is the kind of salvation that Jesus challenged us to bring to others.

A Glimpse of Fr. Hayes

Fr. Mike was very special and his unique personality allowed him to get away with much more than anyone else could.

My story has to do with his smoking. After being involved with him for several years, I began to make this announcement to families when they came to make arrangements for their loved ones. I would first ask them where they would like the service held. If they selected Holy Angels, I informed them that there were two things they should know.

First, there are two time zones in this area: Central Standard Time and Fr. Hayes' time. Father's time runs five to ten minutes late.

Next, when they are following the hearse to the cemetery and see a cigarette butt being flung from the window, it does not belong to any of the funeral home staff! Families would roar with laughter at this one.

—Mike Kosloski, Director of Hamlin Hansen Kosloski Funeral Home,
Moose Lake, MN

Sir 3:17–18, 20, 28–29; Heb 12:18–19, 22–24; Luke 14:1, 7–14

Friend, Move Up Higher

A grade-school teacher named Sheila
  got a surprise while installing a reading-skills program
    on her classroom computer.
The program was geared towards her second graders,
  and she hurriedly answered the quiz questions
    as a way of becoming familiar with it.

Suddenly a message appeared on the computer screen:
"Sheila, you seem to be having trouble with these questions.
  Would you like to go to an easier level?"
After that, she answered the questions more carefully!

Today's gospel passage cautions us
  against presumption in religious matters, too.
We have a tendency to equate virtue with respectability.
We pat ourselves on the back
  because we are church-going and law-abiding.

Luke warns us, "Don't be too sure."

Jesus denounced one sin more than any other.
It was not adultery,
    or theft,
    or pornography,
    or abortion.
It was religious pride.

He most vehemently condemned religious leaders,
  because they didn't see their own need for God.

Most of us abhor pomposity
    and take a perverse delight
    in anything that makes pompous people look ridiculous.
It sometimes seems that Jesus
    upset the religious assumptions of every religious person in Palestine.
He gave comfort to corrupt tax collectors and adulterers
    and condemned priests and Pharisees

He went after the religious establishment with a vengeance.

Like it or not, we are part of today's religious establishment.
We are part of a church, not a movement, and it has its liabilities.
We lack the freshness and energy
    that characterized the early days of Christianity as recorded in Acts.
While they added to their number day by day,
    we are more or less in a holding pattern.

They got in trouble because they upset the social order.
People pass us by because we seem predictable and boring.
We have tamed the gospel
    and the liturgy
    and drained the faith of excitement.
This may be our greatest sin.

It is possible to take something earthshaking and make it humdrum
—and we have done it.

Oh, we have our conversion moments
    when we are filled with the wonder of our faith.
We know we are loved by God
    and enjoy time spent in prayer.
We sense God's presence.

Then other times we feel nothing.
We become numb and preoccupied
    and hope church services won't last a minute longer
    than is absolutely necessary.

Our prayer becomes automatic, and our participation is lifeless.
We grow somewhat oblivious to the things that delighted us before.

Today's gospel is not about where we should sit in church.
Front seats are often the last to be taken!
Rather, it is about knowing our need for God.

We can come and go through the motions
    out of a sense of obligation,
    or we can come with an awareness of our brokenness,
    our blindness,
    and our pride.
We can come with a need to recover the joy and spontaneity in our lives.

We never know what God has in store for us.
We will never discover it
    if we walk around half-dazed and unresponsive.
We must always assume
    we have enormous room for spiritual growth
        and that God will help us find it.

It is the needy,
    not the proud and complacent,
    to whom the host will surely say,
        "Friend, move up higher." (Luke 14:10)

Wis 9:13–18b; Philem 9–10, 12–17; Luke 14:25–33

Discipleship: A Costly Grace

"Whoever does not carry the cross and follow me
   cannot be my disciple." (Luke 14:27)

During the last years of his life,
   French artist Auguste Renoir was virtually crippled by arthritis.
Nevertheless he painted every day.
When his fingers were no longer supple enough
   to hold the brush correctly,
   he had his wife, Alice, attach the paintbrush to his hand
   in order to continue his work.

A friend visited him daily.
One day as he watched his friend
   wincing in excruciating pain with each color stroke,
   he asked,
   "Auguste, why do you continue to paint
      when you are in such agony?"
Renoir's response was immediate,
   "The beauty remains, the pain passes."

He painted until the day he died.
The beauty remains of his smiling portraits,
   his landscapes, and his still-life flowers and fruits.

All agree; the cost was worth it.

Wise teacher that he was,
    Jesus advised his disciples
    that following him would also require
    that they be willing to pay certain costs
        for the sake of what will remain:
            a lasting relationship with him
            and a partnership of shared service
            for the sake of the kingdom.

In today's gospel, Jesus detailed some of the costs of discipleship.
He invited his own
    to value their union with him above and before all other unions.

"Whoever comes to me
    and does not hate father and mother,
    wife and children, brothers and sisters,
    yes, and even life itself, cannot be my disciple." (Luke 14:26)

There was indeed this kind of rupture
    when the first Christians left behind their pagan environment.
Today, however, as followers of Jesus
    we are not required to turn our backs on our families;

Instead we should think of
    what price we are willing to pay
        to be people of good conscience and committed to the gospels.

Jesus counseled his disciples
    against a naïve and starry-eyed commitment
        that was uninformed and unprepared for what lay ahead.

The demands of love are sometimes shocking, too.
Unfortunately today, too many young people
    who enter into marriage
    in the euphoria of romance,
    find themselves unable to meet
    the demands of a lifelong commitment.

In the same way, counting the cost of commitment to Christ
is necessary to remain faithful.

Jesus wanted his own
to be sensitive, sensible, and sober
when it came to calling themselves his followers.

In other words,
Jesus was challenging his disciples
to forego what Dietrich Bonhoffer, author of *The Cost of Discipleship*
described as "cheap grace,"
in favor of costly grace.

Costly grace
is the gospel that must be lived and preached.
It is the gift that must be asked for,
the door at which every disciple must knock.
This grace must be daily appropriated,
and therein lies the cost.

Costly grace means following Jesus,
aware of and prepared for the pitfalls of discipleship
but still willing to meet them and manage them daily.

Jesus challenges us to make our decisions with our eyes wide open.

A young, brilliant scholar and preacher
was asked to speak at an exclusive club in London.
He stood up after an eloquent introduction
and his first words were,
"Gentlemen,
the entrance fee to the kingdom of God is nothing;
the annual subscription is everything."

Ex 32:7–11, 13–14; 1 Tim 1:12–17; Luke 15:1–32 or 15:1–10

It's Not Fair!

"Yet you have never given me even a young goat
    so that I might celebrate with my friends." (Luke 15:29)

"It's not fair!" is heard from the back seat of the car
    when the squabbling siblings argue over a seat by the window.

"It's not fair!" is the cry from the funeral home
    when someone we love dies too young.

Why isn't life fair?
Why do some people get the breaks while others get broken?

Why do some people live long, healthy lives
    while eating fried foods,
    while others die young
    even though they exercised regularly
        and ate only bran and raw vegetables?
It just isn't fair, is it?!

Let's look more closely at the gospel.
We may have a surprise in store.
God does not give any of us what we deserve in life.
God gives us more.

In the gospel lesson today,
Jesus told the immortal story of the prodigal son
    who received grace and was welcomed home with a party
    from the very father he had scorned.

Did this son get what he deserved? Of course not.
The elder son did not get what he deserved either.

Although the older son complained bitterly to the merciful Father
    for the "unfairness" of grace extended to the sinful younger brother,
    the elder brother revealed in his complaining
        that his motives had not been pure either.

Though he had stayed at home,
    his heart was in a far country from the merciful heart of his father.

All he could think of was his preference for "his friends,"
    the party he thought he deserved from his father,
    and the greed that caused him to calculate the inheritance
        before his father's death.

When the older brother refused to attend the party of grace
    for his younger brother,
    the father should have come outside
        and given him a stern sermon or worse.

Instead, the father loves both of his sinful sons.
And the parable ends with the father
    out in the cold, urging the older brother
    to join in the joy meant for them both.

So it is true that life is not fair.
We do not get what we deserve.
We get more.
That is the reason we thank God that he has not given us justice.

Aren't you glad that all of us live and die
    in the hands of a God
    who loves mercy so much
    that he even violates the universal desire for "fairness."

Allow me the following observations.

No matter how many times we leave the father's house
  and get lost,
    he is there for us, inviting us to return home.

The sheep who was lost probably had a propensity to wander off,
    and more than likely wandered off again a second time.

The woman who lost a coin would probably search hard for other coins
    that might get lost in the dusty floors of her home.
She will sweep again to find them.

The prodigal son probably had another chance
    to lose favor with his father,
      even though he had been forgiven earlier by him.

No matter how often the sheep is lost, the coin is lost, the son is lost,
    the unconditional love of our merciful God
      is there to welcome them.

The sheep is not told in so many words,
    "If you get lost again,
      you are headed for the barbeque."

The coin is not told,
    "If you get lost again,
      I'm not going to go looking for you."

And the son is not told,
    "If you wander off again,
      don't bother coming back."

Life is not fair at all.

Thanks be to God.

Amos 8:4–7; 1 Tim 2:1–8; Luke 16:1–13 or 16:10–13

You Owe Me One

"When will the new moon be over
   so that we may sell grain;
   and the sabbath so that we may offer wheat for sale?
We will make the ephah small and the shekel great
   and practice deceit with false balances." (Amos 8:5)

Even in the time of the prophet Amos,
   there were those who manipulated the oil and grain market,
   tampered with the scales,
   rigged the exchange rate,
      all so that they could grow rich at the expense of the poor.

Today we have OPEC, the Organization of Petroleum Exporting Countries.
The man who managed OPEC's rise to power was Sheik Yamani,
   the most dominant of oil ministers.
Yamani, who held the position for twenty-four years,
   engineered the 1973 oil embargo
   which jacked up world oil prices tenfold.

But in October of 1986, the King of Saudi Arabia
   abruptly and dramatically removed Yamani from his post.
Yamani had reportedly been discounting Saudi oil.

The dismissal sounds very much like today's gospel
   concerning "a rich man who had a manager."
The manager learned that he was going to lose his job
   so he offered attractive discounts of up to fifty percent
   to the people who were in debt to the boss.

What a windfall for the people in debt!

The gospel parable let the dishonesty pass for a moment,
so that we can focus on the industry and energy of the dishonest manager.

The dishonest manager knows how to use his head.
He thinks, he plans, and he schemes
    to get personal advantage out of a sticky situation.

His ruse is to write off debts while still in power.
The customer is pleased with the discount.
All the manager does is reduce the amount of the excess padding
    that he had added when the deal had been struck in the first place.

This stroke of genius leaves the master with his money
    and the debtors grateful.
All that was lost was the manager's kickback
    and he bought the goodwill of the debtors with it.

That's the way to make friends with the customers
    so that when he loses his job,
    he'll have some friends in business.
He'll just go back with the line,
    "You owe me one."

Jesus is not only pointing out the outrageous actions of the manager,
    but he is encouraging his followers to focus on the kingdom of God
        with the same zeal as the manager showed in saving his skin!

The point of the parable is that we who want to belong to the kingdom
    could copy the energy of the dishonest manager
        and bring the same shrewdness to our honest pursuits.

Everyday there are untold opportunities
    to grow in our love for God and our neighbor,
    if only we would focus on them
        with the same energy and determination
            as the dishonest manager.

Opportunities to extend our love into the kingdom of God are everywhere.
They are around us at work,
    at school,
    within our extended family,
    the community,
    and the Church.

It is up to us to be just as industrious as the manager
    and find these opportunities to serve one another this week.

Who will be the one saying,
    "You owe me one"?

Amos 6:1a, 4–7; 1 Tim 6:11–16; Luke 16:19–31

You Can't Take It with You

Did you ever see a hearse pulling a U-Haul?

Perhaps this comical image is meant to carry the same impact
    and to serve the same function as did Jesus' parables.
By presenting his listeners with a familiar story, situation, or idea,
    Jesus was able to move them to think about deeper
    and more significant realities,
    and ultimately help his listeners to a change of heart and mind.
He is asking them for conversion
    to his way and his truth.

Through the parable of the rich man and the beggar Lazarus,
    Jesus invited those who heard him
        to re–evaluate the importance they placed on earthly possessions.
Recall that many were inclined to regard material wealth
    as a blessing from God for the righteous.
Conversely they believed that poverty and sickness
    were the deserved lot of sinners.
But Jesus had come to rewrite that script.

In this regard, Jesus' parable reveals a dramatic reversal.
In the afterlife,
    the rich man would know torment
        while the poor man would enjoy abundance.

Surprised, no doubt, by this reversal,
    those who heard Jesus that day,
    and we who hear him again today,
    are confronted with his truth.

For those who would be his disciples,
   wealth should be understood
      neither as a blessing nor as a reward,
   but as an opportunity for doing good.

The maddening thing about the story
   of the rich man and Lazarus in today's gospel,
   is that Jesus never tells us exactly why the rich man went to hell.
He has Abraham say to the man in his torment,
"Remember that during your lifetime you received your good things."
   (Luke 16:25)

But check through any exhaustive catalogue of sins,
   and you will not find "receiving good things" as a serious sin.

The rich man's final destiny obviously had something to do with Lazarus,
   who so indelicately decorated his doorstep.
But in the course of the story,
   Jesus gives us no interaction between the two.
The only contact between the rich man and Lazarus
   is through the rich man's dogs.

The dogs seem to be acting
   on some perverse canine sense of comforting,
      by licking the beggar's sores.

With this story Jesus tells us
   that when the rich stay rich,
   and the poor stay poor,
   and the twain never meet,
   then the rich are in big trouble.

That is because there is another character in this story
   who is never mentioned:
   God.
He is the God of Lazarus,
   but he also wants to be the God of the rich man.

Because the rich man never met Lazarus,
   he never met God.

What would Jesus have had the rich man do?
Ruin himself so he could help all the Lazaruses in his city?
No.

A hint of the solution Jesus is aiming at
   appears in the rich man's request
      that Abraham send Lazarus back from the dead to his family
      to warn them of the consequences of their way of life.

Abraham refuses the Lazarus mission
   and cites the sufficient warnings already given by Moses and the prophets.
The expression simply means the Scriptures.
It is then the rich man blurts out,
"No, father Abraham;
   but if someone goes to them from the dead, they will repent."
   (Luke 16:30)

This is the key word that explains what Jesus is getting at is: Repentance.

Our literature already offers us a story
   of a rich man who neglected the poor
   and, when visited by the dead,
   ultimately repents.
That story is *A Christmas Carol* by Charles Dickens.

What Jesus would have the rich man do first is
   not change Lazarus
   but change himself.
Once this was done, everything else would have followed.
The rich man would have started working on the problem,
   one Lazarus at a time.
No matter how rich we may be or how poor,
   the first step is open to all of us.

Repent...then you see.

Repent...and you will not be able to overlook.

Repent...and you will not need a visitation from beyond the grave
   to see what is under your nose.

Diogenes, the philosopher, was very poor.

One day the Emperor visited him and said,

"You can have anything you wish."

Diogenes said,
   "I wish you to move two steps,
   as you are blocking the sunlight."

Come to think of it,
   have you ever seen a trailer hitch on a hearse?

A Glimpse of Fr. Hayes

Fr. Mike would often ride in the hearse with me to the cemetery. He would jump in, immediately light up a cigarette, and begin telling jokes along the way. One time he told a hilarious story that caught me completely by surprise at the witty punch line. He slapped me on the back and roared with his deep laughter. I laughed so hard that I could barely keep the hearse under control. I could only imagine what the people behind us thought as I wove the hearse back and forth across the road trying to regain my composure!

—Mike Kosloski, Director of Hamlin Hansen Kosloski Funeral Home,
Moose Lake, MN

Hab 1:2–3, 2:2–4; 2 Tim 1:6–8, 13–14; Luke 17:5–10

LORD, INCREASE OUR FAITH

The apostles came to Jesus and said,
    "Lord, increase our faith." (Luke 17:5)

Apparently they had come to recognize the importance of faith
    by seeing it demonstrated in the life of Jesus.
They were saying in effect,
    "We want that same kind of faith in our lives."

First, Jesus made a statement about the power of faith
    when he compared it to the size of a mustard seed.

Second, he tells a little story
    that starts with a question,
    implies an answer,
    and ends with an application.

The question:
    Is a master grateful to his servants for just carrying out orders?
The implied answer is "no."
The application has to do with our relationship to Christ.

He says that when we have done our duty
    and nothing more,
    we should regard ourselves as unworthy servants.

Now keep in mind
    that Jesus said this in response to a request for increased faith.
He seems to be saying
    that increased faith does not come from wishing
        or even from asking.

Increased faith comes from increased living,
    from giving more to life than is required.

If we have a get-by approach to life,
    then we will have a get-by kind of faith.
How could it be otherwise?

Why should we have maximum faith for minimum living?

What does this say to you? To me?
Jesus, in effect, told the disciples
    that faith was not something to be handed out on a platter.
The quality of our faith
    depends on the quality of our living.
If we would have a great faith,
    we must go beyond the call of duty.
We must be willing to give to life
    more than the minimal requirements.

People who spend all their lives in the foothills,
    do not need the kind of faith that is required to climb mountains.

In every area of life,
    the more we expend ourselves,
    the more our confidence increases,
    and the greater our faith becomes.

Take a look at your level of confidence in any area of life.
Where is your faith strongest?
Is it not in that area where you have given the most of yourself?
If you have spent twenty years of your life in the kitchen
    planning menus and preparing meals,
    you can face that experience of life with unshakable faith.
You have been there.
You know what is required
and you know you can handle it.

The same is true of building a house, giving a homily, or making a dress.
The more we have given of ourselves, the greater our faith has become.

Why should it be any different in the realm of the spiritual?

All our experiences of God work that way.
The more we give of ourselves,
    the stronger our faith becomes.
Do you know who the people are
    who believe the most in the power of God
    and worry the least abut the necessities of life?

It is not necessarily the people with the most money.
It's the people who are most involved in meeting the needs
    of our sisters and brothers.

The same is true about the power of God to heal a broken heart.
The people who have the strongest faith in the comforting presence of God
    are the people who are most involved in comforting the bereaved.

Would you like to have an unshakable faith in God
    and a confident faith in others?
Then get involved in life.
Go beyond the call of duty.
Give more of yourself than the minimal requirement,
    and you will discover what Jesus told the apostles:
        Increased faith comes through increased living.

2 Kings 5:14–17; 2 Tim 2:8–13; Luke 17:11–19

In All Circumstances, Give Thanks

"My words fly up,
my thoughts remain below:
Words without thoughts
Never to heaven go."
—William Shakespeare, *Hamlet*

Our eternal salvation
    depends on whether or not we are really thankful.
This is why we celebrate this liturgy together today,
    to give thanks.

How often have we spoken these words of thanksgiving?
In a few moments just before the Preface today, I will say,
    "Let us give thanks to the Lord, our God."
    "It is right to give him thanks and praise."

Then as your spokesperson I will say:
    "He took bread and when he had given thanks."

And then I will say:
"When supper was ended he took the cup.
    Again he gave you thanks and praise."

Giving thanks to God
is the essence of today's liturgy and today's readings.
It is our acknowledgment that God is not an impersonal God,
    but a God who cares.

I do a lot of meditating in truck stops.

Here is an observation.
The "tip" was originally a way of saying thanks;
    thank you to someone who had performed a service
        over and above what was expected.
But now it has become an expectation, an additional charge
    that has no relation to the quality of the service given.
The giver can feel resentful at being forced to leave a tip.
    The receiver often expects it as a right,
        management regards it as part of the salary.

Very often, personal thanks has been lost.
People really need to experience personal thanks.
Sometimes when you thank someone, they say,
    "Don't mention it."
However, they are really glad you mentioned it.

It is very difficult to sustain a strong friendship
    with someone who will not let you thank him or her.

Living a life of gratitude is not always easy.
I have a theory that as the lepers ran on ahead of Jesus to find a priest,
    one of them noticed
        that he had been freed of the dreaded disease along the way.
He was overcome with gratitude and turned to run back to Jesus.
You can just imagine some of the disciples backing away
    when they saw him coming right back at them!

"Praise God, praise God, thank you, Lord," he shouted.
He sobbed, looking up at Jesus through tear-filled eyes.

This man gave personal thanks.
He decided that if he had gone to the priest,
    Jesus would have left.
By the time he had gone through all the red tape,
    all he could have done
        was send the equivalent of a thank you note or an e-mail.
Jesus asks him, "Were not ten of you made clean?
    But the other nine; where are they?" (Luke 17:17)

There has always been a lot of speculation and hunches
    as to why the other nine did not return.

Martin Bell, in his book *The Way of the Wolf*,
    sets out the possible excuses of the nine lepers
        who did not return to thank Jesus for their cure.
Here is a bit of a summary of his hunches.

The first leper was simply too scared.
He was grateful enough but too frightened to say so;
    Jesus scared him.

The second one didn't like the idea of being cured so easily.
He was of the opinion that one should earn a reward.
He thought this was too easy and didn't want spiritual handouts.
No paternalism for him.

The third one came to the painful awareness
    that he liked the pain and humiliation of being a leper
    and attained his enjoyment by wallowing in his misery.
Jesus had taken away his security blanket.

The fourth one was simply so happy about what happened
    that he forgot to come back and say thanks.
A little light-headed and slightly naive, of course,
    but ecstasy does that to some people.

The fifth one had been patronized so often by people
    that he couldn't bear to say thank you to the do-gooders.
He hated the look in their eyes that asked for appreciation.
They were more interested in feeling good themselves
    than in helping him.

The sixth one was a wife and mother.
For years she dreamed about restoration to her family.
She was not ungrateful,
    but her homing instinct and craving for her family
        pushed her to rush home.

The seventh one was an agnostic.
He simply didn't believe in miracles.
Somehow this was an explainable event.
No need to thank Christ for a miracle.

It was the eighth leper's faith that prevented him.
He knew Christ had cured him.
He felt his gratitude would be best expressed
    by going in all directions to tell everyone the good news.
Best to let everyone know.

The excuse of the ninth leper remains a puzzle.
No one will ever quite know.
He gave no clues.
He looked pleased enough.
Felt himself all over.
Looked at his reflection in a pond and just muttered a bit and drifted away.

Sometimes we don't know a person's reasons.
All along we have assumed that the nine lepers were an ungrateful lot.
It's been so easy to assign a negative interpretation and judge the other nine.
Could we possibly have been unfair to them?
    Does God deserve to be thanked? Of course.
    Does God insist on it? Of course not.
"When the giver insists thanks be said,
    the gold in the gift turns to lead."

Jesus knew what happened to the other nine.
When he says, "But the other nine, where are they?"
    he had that all-knowing smile in his eyes.

As Jesus asks us today,
"Were not ten baptized? But the other nine, where are they?"
We believe he knows the reasons
    and carries the all-knowing smile in his eyes once again.

Ex 17:8–13; 2 Tim 3:14—4:2; Luke 18:1–8

Do Not Lose Heart

History says, Don't hope
On this side of the grave.
But then, once in a lifetime
The longed for tidal wave
Of justice can rise up,
And hope and history rhyme.

So hope for a great sea–change
On the far side of revenge.
Believe that a further shore
Is reachable from here.
Believe in miracles
And cures and healing wells.
—Seamus Heaney, "The Cure at Troy"

In today's gospel, Jesus reminds us
    that we need to pray always and not lose heart.
However, we usually begin to pray when our spirit is raw.
    We have an ache, a memory will not go away,
    a sin, or cancer will not go into remission,
    an injustice simply cannot be tolerated.

Then having exhausted our own resources,
    we cast our prayer into the void
        like throwing stones into a bottomless pit,
        or driving golf balls into a lake,
waiting for some response or at least an echo, an echo, an echo…an ache.

We should not be puzzled by the grand silence.

When the finite attempts to rouse the infinite,
   the results are iffy at best.

And yet, we must communicate with God,
   the source of our life.
Activists that we are,
   we presume that it is our business to call God to the conference table.

Not so; God is always present to us.
What we call prayer is simply our occasional response to God's presence.

God is first present to us in the world,
   where he proves that life is good in spite of evil,
   that although we do not have a lasting home in this world,
   all will be well in the end.

God is next present to us in other people
   and there God convinces that trust is often rewarded,
   that hatred need not be fatal,
   that mistakes are reparable,
   that intimacy is possible,
   that our love for each other
      is only a shadow of God's love for us.

And God finally speaks to us in our own selves,
   in our physical talents,
   in the good and bad things that happen to us,
   in the uplifting and awful things we do.

Most intimately God speaks to the Spirit in us,
   where God keeps fondly repeating our name,
   which is our true self.

Just as God once spoke the name Jesus,
   and left nothing else to be said,
   so God speaks our names
   and there is nothing else to say about us.

All our prayers are an attempt to faithfully echo back to God
    the name God fervently keeps repeating to us,
    "By name I have called you."

In fumbling for the various nuances of our name,
    we pray in reaction to God's action on us.

God the creator amazes us
    with galactic fireworks,
    with majestic mountains,
    with innumerable species,
    with microscopic marvels.
We stand in awe with our mouths wide open
    and offer a prayer of adoration.

God the benefactor overwhelms us with life,
    with friends,
    with possessions,
    with work
    with play,
    with purpose.
We stand in gratitude
    and offer a prayer of thanksgiving.

God the forgiver discounts our faults,
    forgets our evil,
    forgives our sins.
We stand in sorrow
    and offer a prayer of reparation.

God the provider has an eye for our spiritual and material needs.
Confident in God's kindness,
    we offer a prayer of petition.

When we pray, we are not asking God to interfere;
    he is always present, feverishly active.
Our prayer adds a new piece to the puzzle.

It gives God something else to work with
    and a new space to operate in.

It is the same with us.
When we ask for a date, or a raise, or the salt,
we are inviting people to expand the area of their relationship with us.

The mere asking alters that relationship.
It shows we trust them.
It makes us vulnerable to refusal.

When we ask God, our very asking deepens our intimacy.
By asking for the least thing,
    we confess that God has the power to make a difference in our lives
    and in the lives of those who trust in God.

We do not know what God does with our prayer,
    any more than we know what God does without our prayer.
We do know that the yearning for prayer
    brings us to a deeper intimacy with the source of life.

"God is closer to you than the beating of your own heart." —The Koran

Sir 35:12–14, 16–18; 2 Tim 4:6–8, 16–18; Luke 18:9–14

What a Good Boy Am I!

"If no change occurs as a result of prayer, then one has not really prayed."
—Raymond Brown

In the gospel today, we hear the parable of the Pharisee
    who went up to the temple to pray.
It is a classic tale of one who trusted himself
    as righteous and regarded others with contempt.

A number of years ago, in Charlotte, North Carolina,
    Judge Robert Potter was not impressed
    when televangelist Jim Bakker told the judge,
    "I have sinned. I've made mistakes."

Judge Potter lived up to his nickname "Maximum Bob"
    by sentencing Bakker to forty-five years in prison
    and a half-million dollar fine.
In handing down the sentence, Judge Potter said,
    "Those of us who do have religion
        are sick of being saps for money-grabbing preachers and priests."

It's a good thing that Maximum Bob wasn't in the temple
    the day the Pharisee went up there to pray.
The Pharisee never would have had a chance.
Maximum Bob would have pointed out
    what preachers have done for centuries:
    how all Pharisees are phonies;
    how the Pharisee was in the front of the temple praying
        not to God but to himself.

Maximum Bob would have told us
    how real religious people stay in the back of the temple,

beating their breasts and centering only on their sins.
"Maximum Bob, wait just a minute!
Let's go back into the temple
    and see and hear what really happened that day."

You can be sure
    that there were more than two people at prayer in the temple.
The place was filled with devout Jews.
It was the custom to go to the temple three times a day to pray:
    9:00 AM, noon, and 3:00 PM.

It's easy to pick on this one Pharisee who prayed like little Jack Horner.
"What a good boy am I!"

But that doesn't mean that all the Pharisees were praying that way.
The temple was filled with other Pharisees
    who prayed not to themselves but honestly to God.
Religious people don't have exclusive rights to phoniness.
And anyway, why do we assume that the Pharisee prayed in the front
    and the tax collector prayed in the back of the temple?

The only thing Luke says in the parable
    is that the tax collector was "standing far off."

He couldn't have been that far away from the Pharisee
    who noticed him when he thanked God
    that he wasn't like "this tax collector."

When we miss this point,
    we continue the tradition of some back-pew Catholics
    who, in an ironic way, think they are less phony
        than the folks up front.

There is an old Irish saying that captures this myth nicely:
    "Never trust anybody in the front pew."

But if we make that judgment,

we miss the heart of this parable.
We all stand in need of God because all of us,
    those up front and those in the back,
    those wearing miters and those wearing baseball caps,
        have been phony to some extent in our dealings with one another.

We are complex.
Walt Whitman said it well, "I am large; I contain a multitude."

There is saint and sinner in each of us,
    and that is the person Jesus is calling us to recognize.
He is not telling us to beat our breasts and dwell only on our phoniness.
He is not telling us to judge all religious people as phony.
He is calling all of us to stand before God in honesty.

The gospel tells us that Jesus never found it difficult
    to determine who his audience was when he prayed
        in the temple, on the road, even on the cross;
    he prayed honestly to God.
The prayers of Jesus remind us
    that since God knows no favorites,
    there's no reason to fake it.

"Prayer doesn't change God, but it changes the one who prays."
                        —Søren Kierkgaard

Wis 11:22—12:2; 2 Thess 1:11—3:2; Luke 19:1–10

he Knows My Name!

"For the Son of Man came to seek out and to save the lost." (Luke 19:10)

On this Lord's day, God gathers us together
    and reminds us through the gospel story of Zacchaeus
    that Jesus comes to seek and save the lost.
If we feel spiritually lost, searching for direction in life,
    today's liturgy can speak to our hearts.

Zacchaeus was a man small in stature
    and unable to see Jesus through the crowds of taller people.
In his excitement and curiosity about seeing the Lord,
    he set out running far ahead of Jesus.
He found an old sycamore tree, climbed it,
    and worked his way out to the center spot over the road.
Looking back down, Zacchaeus was happy to see that Jesus
    and his followers were coming straight for him.

What a marvelous story of ingenuity!
It shows us that sometimes, for whatever reason,
    our ability to see the Lord may be blocked, too.

A belt of fear knifed into the tax collector
    as the eyes of Jesus locked with his own.
"Zacchaeus, hurry and come down,
    for I must stay at your house today." (Luke 19:5)

Zacchaeus reeled, almost losing his grip on the support branch.
He held on hard, stunned by the realization that "he knows my name!"

It is both fearsome and wondrous to realize that Jesus knows our name.
Our creator who has breathed us into life
   and filled us with his love,
   sets the meter for our heartbeats,
   and walks us through life.
Yet like Zacchaeus, we are surprised that he knows our names.

Even more surprising is that as unworthy as we may think ourselves to be,
      he would choose to come and stay with us.

Jesus is now drawing near to the end of his journey toward Jerusalem.
Throughout this journey
   we have heard stories of the lost sheep, the lost coin, the lost son.
Each of these stories tells of great rejoicing
   with friends and neighbors, with lavish feasting
   to celebrate the restoration of those who have been lost.

Celebration always follows all conversion of heart.
We can only imagine what the subsequent meal was like
   that Jesus and Zacchaeus then shared.

The charm of the story lies in its portrayal of a man
   so eager to see Jesus that he throws aside all dignity
   by running, climbing, and clawing his way to Jesus,
   who responds immediately with compassion.

Jesus did not condone his crimes, but he had compassion for him.
Despite the complaints of the "respectable,"
   Jesus and Zacchaeus go into the feast joyfully, together.
They eat with good conscience.

Like all good stories,
   this one reflects something of our own reality back to us.
If we listen carefully,
   we will hear Jesus' gracious and loving demand
      to enter our house today.
Let us go into this lavish feast joyfully, together.

2 Macc 7:1–2, 9–14; 2 Thess 2:16—13:15; Luke 20:27–38

A God of Life

"Now he is God not of the dead, but of the living." (Luke 20:38)

As Advent approaches, the liturgy calls us
    to feel our need for salvation,
    to look for a light to follow,
    to find hope in our dark times.

Let me suggest that the almost comical story,
    the gospel story of the woman with seven different husbands,
    offers at least a sliver of hope and light as we close this Church year.

Here's how.
Jesus, when asked how soap-opera type human relations in this life
    will be sorted out "in the resurrection,"
    he answers not specifically but reassuringly,
    that the God of Abraham, of Isaac and Jacob
        is a God of life, not death.
They needn't worry about such human conundrums.

Both the doomed Maccabees and Jesus clung to a God of life.
No doubt every human life will hold suffering,
    confusion, uncertainty, and darkness.
That same God of life is with us, too,
    during both unspeakable suffering and unbridled joy.

As we prepare for Advent and a new Church year,
    the terrifying story from the Hebrew Testament,
    the frightening stories of our own world,
    and the pain in our own lives,
    are where we need to start.

Our violent culture and the challenges of this world
    need the light and hope that we as Christians can bring.

This is the time of year we are reminded
    to let this light and hope of the resurrection become real enough
    so that we live not in despair,
    but in the light, life and hope
        that the God of life provides.

We once again seek
    to understand, accept and see contemporary meaning
    in the Word made flesh.

As we approach the new Church year and move
    from darkness to light,
    from despair to hope,
    from pain to joy,
let's allow just a little more of this divine presence,
    a gift from the God of life,
        to take root in our lives.

Mal 3:19–20a; 1 Thes 3:7–12; Luke 21:5–19

You Are Still You, and I Love You

"There will be great earthquakes,
    and in various places famines and plagues." (Luke 21:10)

In 1906, the city of San Francisco was virtually destroyed
    because of a powerful earthquake.
Afterwards, religious spokesmen began to interpret the disaster
    in terms of divine judgment.
They drew parallels between San Francisco
    and the biblical cities of Sodom and Gomorrah.
Also, they predicted that this was the beginning of the end of the world.

But not everyone bought that explanation.
A newspaper reporter, walking through the devastation,
    saw a liquor distillery that had hardly been touched,
    and on the other side of it,
        a church building that had been leveled.

So the man wrote a little verse about it:
    "If, as they say,
    God spanked the town
    For being over-frisky,
    Why did he burn the churches down
    And spare the devil's whiskey?"

The readings of today are difficult
    only because of the apocalyptic style
    which mixes together historic events,
    sayings of Jesus, and a sense of doom.

There are only a few encouraging words added at the end.
"By your endurance you will gain your soul." (Luke 21:19)

A paraphrase of this gospel might go like this:
    You are going to live in troubled times.
There will be natural disasters
    like earthquakes, plagues, famines.
Armies will develop new weapons
    that rain down fire from the sky
        and destroy cities, temples, libraries, museums, everything.

But no matter what happens, do not lose faith in God.
The evils that will come upon the world are of two kinds,
    as evil has always been.
The first is linked to nature, such as the earthquake.
The second comes from the sinful designs of people,
    such as rulers and generals seeking power
        and dictators trampling on human rights.
When these things happen, do not lose faith.
God is still there to sustain you.

There will be persecution of people for political reasons
    but also for their religious beliefs.
In some countries people will be forbidden to worship together,
    even to possess a Bible.
Their missionaries will be forbidden to convert anyone.
Many will die violently.
But in all this, stand firm.
By patient endurance you will save your souls.

The evil events we see flash across our screens on the evening news
    can be devastating, if we don't put them in perspective.
However, this does not have to be "as good as it gets."

But what is enduring?
It seemed to the disciples
    that the Temple of Jerusalem would last forever.

It was to be one of the wonders of the world
 "adorned with beautiful stones and gifts dedicated to God." (Luke 21:5)

Early in the twentieth century,
 a spectacular ship named the Titanic was built to be "unsinkable."
But the Temple was destroyed and the Titanic sunk
 because they are not the sort of things that endure.

The things that truly count in life are
 love, compassion, forgiveness, concern, and understanding.
Let's add joyfulness, playfulness, laughter,
 and the sparkle in the eye of a child, too.

It is comforting to know
 that these are some of the things that endure,
 even beyond the worst of tragedies.
You'll see it in the aftermath of the chaos of natural disasters and war.
The photographers and journalists will be there pointing this out to us.
Gordon Parks, a *Life* photographer, did this masterfully.

The promise of a deep abiding serenity
 is the meaning of Christ's words today.
If important things like love, compassion, forgiveness
 are the things that endure,
 then they should be our primary concern.

We can build a temple, a ship, a business, a fortune
 knowing it can be destroyed.
But instead we need to build love, friendship, a peaceful home,
 knowing that their fruits will endure forever.

Christopher Reeve, popularly known as Superman,
 was severely injured in a riding accident
 shortly after he married his wife, Dana.

In his book *Still Me*, Dana says,
 "I will be with you for the long haul, no matter what."

And then she added the words that saved his life.
"You are still you, and I love you."

When we hear these end time readings
    and ponder the mystery of a second coming and death,
    it is comforting to discover
    that God's unconditional love is saying to us:

"I will be with you for the long haul, no matter what.
    You are still you, and I love you."

2 Sam 5:1–3; Col 1:12–20; Luke 23:35–43

Where Are Your Wounds?

On December 11, 1925, Pope Pius XI instituted the Feast of Christ the King.
It was to be celebrated on the last Sunday of October (not November).
The new feast day was created for political
    as well as theological reasons.
Christ the King was to be a weapon against what the pope described as
    "the destructive forces of our age."

Among the forces were
the Bolshevik Revolution in Russia in 1917,
    the Fascist rise to power in Italy in 1924,
    Hitler's establishment of the Nazi party in Germany in 1925,
    and the rise of materialism across the Atlantic
        during the so-called Roaring Twenties.
The Feast of Christ the King enabled the Church
    to express its censure and anxiety over political developments
        and to represent its stand at that particular moment in time.

As a result of the reforms of the Second Vatican Council,
    the Feast of Christ the King was transferred
        to the last Sunday of November,
    where it acquired a more spiritual
    and coming-again-of-Christ orientation.
This is evidenced in today's readings.

Today, we celebrate the kingship of Jesus
    and renew our allegiance of his reign over us
        with heart, soul, mind, and strength.
We pledge him the allegiance, which is our faith.
We pay homage to him who conquers,
    not by violent arms, but by overbearing love.

His kingdom is the opposite of a "culture of death."
Just as it took a million selfish choices to create this culture of death,
    so it will take another million unselfish choices to create a culture of life.

Miguel Pro was a young Jesuit priest in Mexico.
When Cales, the Mexican President, suppressed all public worship in 1926,
    Fr. Miguel Pro went into hiding,
    but he continued to celebrate Mass and to minister in secret.
In 1927, he was arrested and shot by a firing squad.
Seconds before the command to fire, he raised his voice in a prayerful shout.
His words, "Viva Christo Rey," (Long live Christ the King)
    rang out joyfully across the square, ahead of the gunfire.

"Viva Christo Rey" was a greeting used by the ordinary Mexican people
    who preserved their faith during days of fierce persecution.

"Viva Christo Rey" is a prayer of hope,
    and on this feast we think about our need for hope,
        and the hope Christ gives us.

Alan Paton, the white novelist of black and white South Africa,
    died before he could help shape the liberation of his country,
    but two of his novels *Cry, the Beloved Country*
    and *Too Late the Palapope* were so powerful
        that they surely contributed to the birth of the new nation.

In a third novel written in 1981, *Ah, but Your Land Is Beautiful*,
    one of the characters, Emmanuel, has been terribly hurt in racist violence.
When a companion expresses alarm at his injuries,
    Emmanuel answers, "I don't worry about my wounds.
When I go up there, which is my intention, the Big Judge will say to me,
'Where are your wounds?' and I say, 'I haven't got any,'
    he will say, 'Was there nothing to fight for?'"

The Big Judge did not have to ask for the wounds of Fr. Miguel Pro.
Wasn't it the wounds of the risen Lord that Jesus shared with Thomas?
They are the marks of his victory.

They bear testimony to the fact that he found something to fight for:
　ordinary people, poor people, all people.

Jesus did not engage in armed struggle nor encourage it.
But he did not fear to confront the establishment with a new ethic of love.
In this above all, in his ministry as well as his teaching,
　he conveyed a sense of the worth of everyone.

Force can sometimes serve as a stop-gap,
　but it cannot change the way people think or feel.
It can only temporarily change the way they act.
Nelson Mandela, as a young man, was put in a South African jail
　because of his resistance to the apartheid system.
He stayed there for twenty-seven years,
　to emerge and be elected president of the nation.
All the force that an unjust system could muster
　did not change his mind about justice.

You may be aware of the Chiapas in southern Mexico,
　where a rebellion broke out in 1993, a civil war that still continues.
No one knows the outcome of the struggle.
But if Bishop Ruiz is killed,
　as Archbishop Romero was killed in San Salvador,
　he will have those wounds to show before the King.

We need to be aware of injustice in the world,
　but we should also look around for injustice
　　in our homes, our church, our schools, and community,
　　and be engaged in peaceful efforts to bring about a change.
If the conflict proves difficult, we should still pursue it.
Otherwise, there is some danger
　we will one day appear before the King and hear his question:
　"Where are your wounds?
　　Was there nothing to fight for?"

A Glimpse of Fr. Hayes

There in the dim light of the tree-filtered afternoon, he gave me the news. He was slumped into the curve of his old easy chair, in his rumpled clothes, the smoke from his cigarette seeking the 60-watt lamp light behind him. He hadn't shaved for nearly three weeks. His right eye was sewn shut from his recent surgery. On the floor around him, piles of papers: files, letters, get well cards, hospital bills, clippings from The Irish Times. *The TV flashed behind me, the sound turned off, the usual annoyance.*

"But, the news isn't good," he told me, as though we were in the middle of a two-way conversation. "I have lung cancer."

"Well, can't they operate?" I asked, knowing only too well that he was probably far gone, too far gone for any kind of curative treatment. His pallor all through winter had been alarming.

"No, for some reason it is inoperable. I really won't know until I talk to the guy on Thursday." He held his cigarette in one hand and with the other rubbed over his stubbly face, his eyes squeezed shut. His news had sucked all the energy from the room. It left us in a sort of formal discomfort. He showed no hint of fear or sadness.

Instead of continuing to talk about his cancer, he told me that Holmes, his cat, liked to go out on a leash. Father had the slim, black cord right next to his chair. He picked it up, and Holmes opened an eye, slid up on his feet, and walked nonchalantly over to Father. His hands shook as he slipped the delicate collar over the striped head of his companion. He stood up slowly, unsteadily, and walked with the cat to his back door.

"He likes to be out on it, but he won't be walked," he told me. "So I keep him on this hook." The thin leash and wobbly hook onto which Holmes was tethered would have made for an easy escape, but Holmes never tried. Once the patient cat was secured, Father's shaking hands fell to his sides.

His slim fingers were gray and papery, like an old woman's who had long ago given up housework. On his left hand, he wore a heavy ring of black onyx set in paling gold. The ring looked aristocratic, an heirloom. It suited him. I could picture it moving in the air with his hands when he stood up in the pulpit after the gospel and encouraged us to give in to the love of God in one another, to forgive one another, to forgive ourselves.

I gave him a long hug, and he hugged me back. "Let me know, Shep." I said flatly. I called him "Shep" because he was my Good Shepherd. I told him so, years ago. I don't think he liked the nickname—I don't think he liked nicknames at all—but it just comes to my lips, sometimes. "I will, yes," was his reply.

I drive along the lake and ease left, into the traffic, toward home. The light turns green as I approach and I slide through the last intersection in town, past our new church, and on to the county line road.

Horses and foals graze in the breeze. The fishermen are plying the riffling waters near the culvert on Island Lake. Lilacs bloom, and the woods are full of trillium. They are blushing now, from white to their soft pink, the last stage of their upward life before they die off for the season and go back underground. The sight of them there, in their places, in the westering sun, is enough to make a person forget about being huddled up against winter, and let her mind slip over to thoughts of rebirth, of resurrection in its varying forms.

The idea should be a buoyant one, should smooth the forehead and settle the nerves, like any powerful anesthetic. But just now, it spins down like a dry, lonely leaf that hung on through winter, only to be blown to its end in a tangle of new grass. I decide it might be easier to consider all this another day. I am spent. Yet, I thank God for the gift of my tether to this man, even with this cost. I pray for the patience to be more like Shep and let things work themselves out. Still, I know it will be much harder than it looks.

—Jacinta T. Carlson, parishioner of Holy Angels Church, Moose Lake, MN

Other Feasts
& Occasions

Rev 7:2–3, 9–14; 1 Jn 3:1–3; Mt 5:1–12a

The Torch of Life

After a month-long blitz in preparation for Halloween,
    something is decidedly off-kilter
    if All Saints and All Souls
    are anything but vibrant days of celebration in the parish.

We don't think of Christmas Eve as a holiday separate from Christmas.
So why think of Halloween as something other than the vigil of All Saints?

Some people claim that Halloween is pagan or druid, or even satanic,
    and so it has no business being celebrated by Christians.
Many Halloween traditions in their origins are All Saints/All Souls traditions.
    Our job is to rediscover what is Catholic about All Saints and its Eve.

"Ghoulies and ghosties, and long-legged beasties,
    and things that go bump in the night."

Halloween is a shortened version
    of the Old English form of All Hallows Evening.
It means the eve of All Saints Day.
The Feast of All Saints is centuries old.
It was originally a celebration
    of the nameless martyrs of the Roman persecution.
The feast was particularly popular in England
    where it was known as All Hallows.
But the eve of this feast
    was celebrated long before it came to the British Isles and Ireland.

There it took on the distinguished coloring we associate with it today.
Pre-Christian England believed that the souls of the dead
    returned to their former villages and homes one night a year.

The living set out gifts of food for them
    to avoid the mischief they might otherwise cause.

So when little boys and girls, "ghosts and goblins,"
    go out to trick or treat
        they are re-enacting this ancient ritual of death.

We modern Americans, it is said,
    have pretty well insulated ourselves from death.
In American culture,
    death is something that takes place in hospitals and nursing homes.
We cosmetize it in a way our ancestors never dreamed of.
One reason why death may have been more familiar to them
    was that few of them lived very long.

There is no place in Christian belief for ghosts and goblins,
    but we do reverence the dead.
We do that for many reasons.
The first reason is simple.
Were it not for them we would not be here at all.
We live in the land that once was theirs,
    sometimes in the very house they lived in.
We swim in their lakes, fish in their streams, and walk in their woods.

We carry on many of their customs.
We celebrate Thanksgiving and Memorial Day as they did.
Most likely we are Christian and Catholic because they were.
The early immigrants to the United States built the vast infrastructures
    that included the diocese, the parish,
        the church that we take for granted.

Evolutionary psychology is beginning to suspect
    that many of our spontaneous reactions
    are part of our genetic heritage.
If we tend to worry,
    it is very likely that our remote ancestors worried a good deal.
The worriers tended to survive.

A quarter million generations separate us from our pre-history ancestors.
As we pause to think of them,
    we must marvel that the torch of life
    somehow passed from one to another
        of those thousands of generations until it reached us.

We may be stunned to realize
    how briefly we are allowed to hold this torch of life
        before we, too, pass it on.
We may be a bit more conscious of our own priorities,
    a little more aware of what is really important,
    a bit more conscious of the injunction of Jesus,
    "Lay out treasure for yourself in heaven."

All things considered,
    Halloween really can supply us with food for thought.

Where have all the saints gone?
Are there saints today?

There are thousands, perhaps millions,
    and we are fortunate enough to know a few
        whose lives inspire us and mirror God.
They reflect the divine goodness.

Recently a striking ceremony took place
    in Westminster Abbey in London, England.
There had been ten empty niches there,
    but they are now filled with statues
        of those who are called modern-day martyrs.
Below them are figures symbolizing
    truth, justice, mercy, and peace.
Who are these martyrs?

Here are five:
Dietrich Bonhoeffer, German Lutheran minister
    who was killed by the Nazis.

Maximillian Kolbe, Polish Franciscan priest,
    who gave his life to spare another in a Nazi extermination camp.
Martin Luther King, Jr., a Baptist pastor,
    assassinated in 1968.
Janani Livuum, an Anglican bishop
    murdered by Idi Amin, the tyrant of Uganda.
Bishop Oscar Romero, killed while saying Mass in 1980,
    gunned down by right-wing forces in the army,
        a martyr to justice and love for the poor.

None were Anglican, but it doesn't matter.

Many think we should take a similar action
    especially with lay people like Cesar Chavez and Dorothy Day.
Many people lead saintly lives but some are heroic.
We remember them,
    take their names,
    and try in our own way to be faithful to the gospel as they were.

Saints and today's liturgy call us to our full potential.
We are called to join the communion of saints.

"Beloved, we are God's children now;
    what we will be has not yet been revealed.
What we do know is this: when he is revealed,
    we will be like him, for we will see him as he is." (1 Jn 3:2)

Gen 3:9–15, 20; Eph 1:3–6, 11–12; Luke 1:26–38

Full of Grace

On this Advent day we gather
    to give honor to Mary, the Immaculate Conception.
It is her chief Advent feast.

This is what we believe about Mary.

Adam and Eve said "no" to God and Mary said "yes."
Mary became a new Eve, a name that means "the mother of life."

One meaning of the word "sin" is "separation from God."
We believe that Mary was never separated from the love of God.

The word "grace" means "gift."
God's gift of grace makes us holy and frees us from sin.
Even before her birth, Mary was filled with grace…full of grace.

What does it mean to be full of grace?
In simple terms, it means to be holy.
And so we say things like,
    "Mary was all pure."
    "Mary was preserved from the stain of original sin."

However, that is not the way holiness is presented in today's gospel.

In the dialogue between the angel Gabriel and Mary,
    what is striking is not how clean Mary was,
    but rather how utterly free she was to respond to God's call.

Nothing held her back from saying "yes" to God.
Nothing.
Not fear…"I'm too scared,"
 nor pride…"Sorry Gabe, but I've made other plans,"
 not even false humility…"Who me? You've got to be kidding!"

No, Mary simply said,
 "Let it be with me according to your word." (Luke 1:38)

What holds me back from responding to God's call in my life?
What keeps me from freely saying "yes?"

Is it fear, pride, false humility? You can fill in the blank.

We need to ask Mary to help us name those things
 that prevent us from being full of grace.
That is our work of Advent as we prepare for Christ's coming.

As Mary gave herself to God,
 so her son gives us all that he is in the Eucharist.
Like her,
 let us open our hands to receive this gift in Communion,
 full of love, life, and grace.

Let us say "yes" and invite Mary to be our companion
 through these days of Advent preparation.

A Wedding Homily

A couple of years ago, I saw the show *Love Letters* in Minneapolis,
    about two people who carry on a lifetime relationship
        by writing letters to each other.

There are only two actors in the show.
    In this case it was Robert Wagner and Stephanie Powers.
They simply read the love letters to each other.
It reminded me a bit of Jim and Therese
    and their "Love Calls" between Washington, Fargo, and later, St. Paul.

    Though the art of letter writing has almost disappeared,
    the homily today is in the form of a letter,
        a love letter to Jim and Therese.

Dear Jim and Therese,

I write this letter to you on your wedding day.
I write because in the midst of all that happens today,
    in the midst of all these good people,
    your family and friends, who came to be with you,
    nothing is more important
    than your desire to be here in this time and place,
    in this community of faith, to proclaim publicly
        that you promise to be as good as God to each other.

I admire your courage more than I admire your love,
    because I believe that before there can be true love,
    there must be true courage.
Like Sarah and Tobit, you begin with prayer.
You understand that what you do here
    is far more important than just a day,
        a wedding is just a day after all,
            but this marriage is for a lifetime.

You understand that what you do here is far more important
    than just for personal convenience.

You understand that what you do here is far more important
    than for the conventions of society.

You understand that the noble purpose of marriage
    has no room for passing fancies,
        nursed wounds, power plays, or bruised egos.

You want us to hear what you say to each other:
"No matter what comes, I will love, I will cherish you.
I will honor you no matter what comes, so help me God."

That is bravery.
You are brave hearts
    and I do not think that kind of courage comes easily…
    nor does it come to everyone.
You two are fortunate.

Do you understand?
This is pure grace, Amazing Grace.
I think you do understand.

I know your story.
From St. Paul, Minnesota, to Washington, DC,
    to Fargo, North Dakota, you were friends.
And then, when your friendship turned deeper,
    there was something still missing.
You knew you had to somehow fashion your love in the image of God.

The faith given to you as children by your parents
    had to grow into adulthood,
        if you are to live out what you promise here today.

On this day, everybody else gives you gifts.
Instead, I have a request to make of you.

For as much as the promises you make today are to each other,
    please understand that you are making these promises to us, too.

You are the salt of the earth.
We need to see your love withstand the strong, cold winds of division.
We need to see your faithfulness prevail against the odds.
We need to see in your words and actions
    how human beings can be as good as God for each other.

You give us hope that with Christ's help we can live at peace with one another.
Your relationship can encourage us in all our trials.
Will you always keep us in mind, not just your family and friends,
    but the whole Church, the people you work with,
    the people you pass on the street?
We need you to show us the courage of loving as Christ did.
To give meaning to the long history of the human race, we need you.
As your Riverdance meets the ocean,
    we expect to see a great sea change.

Finally Jim and Therese, I want you to know you are in my humble prayers as
the priest who witnesses your vows along and with all here present.
    I love you, too.
And I pray that God will always hold the two of you "in the palm of his hand."
That is a safe place to grow old together in your love.

Your friend in love,
Michael T. Hayes

P.S.   *Don't walk ahead of me, I may not follow.*
        Don't walk behind me, I may not lead.
        But walk beside me and be my friend.

—Given for the wedding of
Therese Ann Groh and James Albert Faulconbridge
June 8, 1996